THE MAGUS;

OR,

CELESTIAL INTELLIGENCER.

BOOK II. PART I.

CONTAINING

MAGNETISM,

AND

CABALISTICAL MAGIC;

DISCOVERING

THE SECRET MYSTERIES

OF

CELESTIAL MAGIC.

With the Art of calculating by the divine Names of God; shewing the Rule, Order, and Government of

ANGELS, INTELLIGENCES, AND BLESSED SPIRITS, HOLY TABLES AND SEALS, TABLES OF THE CABALA, &c.

Likewise treating of Ceremonial Magic, Invocation of Spirits, Consecrations, Circles, &c. Also of Dreams, Prophecy, Miracles, &c.

By *FRANCIS BARRETT*,

STUDENT OF CHEMISTRY, NATURAL AND OCCULT PHILOSOPHY, THE CABALA, &c.

TO WHICH IS ADDED,

A Translation of the Works of TRITEMIUS of SPANHEIM, *viz. His Book of Secret Things, and of Spirits.*

BOOK II.

The Magus: Book 2
ISBN 1-58509-032-8

Also Available:

The Magus: Book 1
ISBN 1-58509-031-X

The Magus: The Set
ISBN 1-58509-033-6

Published by
The Book Tree
Post Office Box 724
Escondido, CA 92033

Call (800) 700-TREE for a FREE BOOK TREE CATALOG with over 1000 Books, Booklets, Audio, and Video on Alchemy, Ancient Mysteries, Anti-Gravity, Atlantis, Free Energy, Gnosticism, Health Issues, Magic, Metaphysics, Mythology, Occult, Rare Books, Religious Controversy, Sitchin Studies, Spirituality, Symbolism, Tesla, and much more. Or visit our website at www.thebooktree.com

Orme Del. & Sculp. Engraver to the King &c.

Francis Barrett.

Student in Chemistry, Metaphysicks.

Natural & Occult Philosophy &c &c.

THE MAGUS: BOOK TWO

INTRODUCTION TO BOOK TWO

The Magus has proved to be the most sought after set of books on magic and alchemy ever published. There is very good reason for this. These books are powerful, and were considered so dangerous that for many years, rare copies could only be found in certain libraries, locked away from the general public and from those who would use (or misuse) its power.

The original set of books was first published in 1801 by its author, Francis Barrett, who first spent many years of diligent study before releasing them. His premise for the material, that is, before putting anything into these books, Barrett first subjected the various theories to certain tests that had to be "substantiated by nature, truth, and experiment" first. In other words, the magical practices had to work on a convincing level before Barrett would bother including them. Anything that he considered interesting, but idle speculation, was discounted and not included.

Book Two covers Cabalistic magic, the names of angels and spirits, magnetic powers, healing powers, and ceremonial magic—including the performing of invocations, conjuring spirits, magic circles, receiving oracles in dreams, and positive and evil spirits. The book concludes with a section on the great magicians of history, taken from extremely rare manuscripts at the time of original publication.

This information is not to be used as a toy. It is not a joke. It is spiritually based research—some of which makes little sense on a logical or practical level—but in many cases it works. Concentration and good intentions are essential elements for success, and people embarking on this "journey" should not consider it lightly and jump in and "play around." Although outer results may be apparent, this is inner work. If not done properly, meaning if these things are not done with good intent, it will "mess you up" because one will otherwise be attracting elements (or elementals) that do not have good intentions in mind. We all have good and bad within each of us, and the surrounding spirit world is not outside of this general rule. Just because something cannot be seen, doesn't mean that it is completely unable to jump up and bite you in the you know where, if you start poking at it. In other words, do not misuse these books. Treat them with the respect they deserve. If you do, certain things may well manifest which will show respect to you.

Paul Tice

THE MAGUS.

CONTAINING

MAGNETISM,

AND

CABALISTICAL MAGIC.

TO WHICH IS ADDED

A TREATISE

ON

PROPHECY, PROPHETIC DREAMS AND INSPIRATION.

BOOK II. PART I.

MAGNETISM.

IN our following Treatise of Magnetism we have collected and arranged in order some valuable and secret things out of the writings of that most learned chemist and philosopher Paracelsus, who was the ornament of Germany and the age he lived in. Likewise we have extracted the very marrow of the science of Magnetism out of the copious and elaborate works of that most celebrated philosopher (by fire) Van Helmont, who, together with Paracelsus, industriously promulgated all kinds of magnetic and sympathetic cures, which, through the drowsiness, ignorance, unbelief, and obstinacy of

the

the present age, have been so much and so totally neglected and condemned ; yet, however impudent in their assertions, and bigotted to their own false opinions, some of our modern philosophers may be, yet we have seen two or three individuals, who, by dint of perseverance, have proved the truth and possibility of Magnetism, by repeated and public experiments. Indeed the ingenious invention of the Magnetic Tractors prove at once that science should never be impeded by public slander or misrepresentation of facts that have proved to be of general utility. And we do not doubt but that we shall be able to shew, by the theory and practice delivered in the sequel, that many excellent cures may be performed by a due consideration and attentive observance of the principles upon which sympathy, antipathy, magnetic attraction, &c. are founded ; and which will be fully illustrated in the following compendium :

We shall hasten to explain the first principles of Magnetism, by examining the magnetic or attractive power.

CHAP. I.

* THE MAGNETIC, OR ATTRACTIVE POWER OR FACULTY.

AS concerning an action locally at a distance, wines do suggest a demonstration unto us : for, every kind of wine, although it be bred out of co-bordering provinces, and likewise more timely blossoming elsewhere, yet it is troubled while our country vine flowereth ; neither doth such a disturbance cease as long as the flower shall not fall off from our vine ; which thing surely happens, either from a common motive-cause of the vine and wine, or from a particular disposition of the vine, the which indeed troubles the wine, and doth shake it up and down with a confused tempest : or likewise, because the wine itself doth thus trouble itself of its own free accord,

* Van HELMONT.

by

by reason of the flowers of the vine : of both the which latter, if there be a fore-touched conformity, consent, co-grieving, or congratulation ; at least, that cannot but be done by an action at a distance : to wit, if the wine be troubled in a cellar under ground, whereunto no vine perhaps is near for some miles, neither is there any discourse of the air under the earth, with the flower of the absent vine ; but, if they will accuse a common cause for such an effect, they must either run back to the stars, which cannot be controuled by our pleasures and liberties of boldness ; or, I say, we return to a confession of an action at a distance : to wit, that some one and the same, and as yet unknown spirit, the mover, doth govern the absent wine, and the vine which is at a far distance, and makes them to talk and suffer together. But, as to what concerns the power of the stars, I am unwilling, as neither dare I, according to my own liberty, to extend the forces, powers, or bounds of the stars beyond or besides the authority of the sacred text, which faith (it being pronounced from a divine testimony) that the stars shall be unto us for signs, seasons, days, and years : by which rule, a power is never attributed to the stars, that wine bred in a foreign soil, and brought unto us from far, doth disturb, move, or render itself confused : for, the vine had at some time received a power of encreasing and multiplying itself before the stars were born : and vegetables were before the stars, and the imagined influx of these : wherefore also, they cannot be things conjoined in essence, one whereof could consist without the other. Yea, the vine in some places flowereth more timely ; and, in rainy, or the more cold years, our vine flowereth more slowly, whose flower and stages of flourishing the wine doth, notwithstanding, imitate ; and so neither doth it respect the stars, that it should disturb itself at their beck.

In the next place, neither doth the wine hearken unto the flourishing or blossoming of any kind of capers, but of the wine alone : and therefore we must not flee unto an universal cause, the general or universal ruling air of worldly successive change ; to wit, we may rather run back unto impossibilities and absurdities, than unto the most near commerces of resemblance and unity, although hitherto unpassable by the schools.

Moreover,

Moreover, that thing doth as yet far more manifestly appear in ale or beer : when, in times past, our ancestors had seen that of barley, after whatsoever manner it was boiled, nothing but an empty ptisana or barley-broth, or also a pulp, was cooked ; they meditated, that the barley first ought to bud (which then they called malt) and next, they nakedly boiled their ales, imitating wines : wherein, first of all, some remarkable things do meet in one ; to wit, there is stirred up in barley, a vegetable bud, the which when the barley is dried, doth afterwards die, and loseth the hope of growing, and so much the more by its changing into meal, and afterwards by an after-boiling, it despairs of a growing virtue ; yet these things nothing hindering, it retains the winey and intoxicating spirit of aqua vitæ, the which notwithstanding it doth not yet actually possess : but at length, in number of days, it attaineth it by virtue of a ferment : to wit, in the one only bosom of one grain one only spirit is made famous with diverse powers, and one power is gelded, another being left : which thing indeed, doth as yet more wonderfully shine forth ; when as the ale or beer of malt disturbs itself while the barley flowereth, no otherwise than as wine is elsewhere wont to do : and so a power at a far absent distance is from hence plain to be seen : for truly there are cities from whom pleasant meadows do expel the growing of barley for many miles, and by so much the more power-fully do ales prove their agreement with the absent flowering barley ; in as much as the gelding of their power hath withdrawn the hopes of budding and in-creasing : and at length the aqua vitæ being detained and shut up within the ale, hogshead, and prison of the cellar, cannot with the safety of the ale or beer wandering for some leagues unto the flowering ear of barley, that thereby, as a stormy retainer, it may trouble the remaining ale with much confusion. Certainly there is a far more quiet passage for a magnetical or attractive agreement among some agents at a far distance from each other, than there is to dream an aqua vitæ wandering out of the ale of a cellar, unto the flower-ing barley, and from thence to return unto the former receptacles of its pen-case, and ale : But the sign imprinted by the appetite of a woman great with child, on her young, doth fitly, and alike clearly confirm a magnetism or attractive faculty and its operation at a distance : to wit, let there be a woman great with child,

which

which desires another cherry, let her but touch her forehead or any other place with her finger; without doubt, the young is signed in its forehead with the image of the cherry, which afterwards doth every year wax green, white, yellow, and at length looks red, according to the tenor of the trees : and it much more wonderfully expresses the same successive alteration of maturities in Spain than in Germany : and so hereby an *action at a distance* is not only confirmed, but also a conformity or agreement of the essences of the cherry tree, in its wooden and fleshly trunk ; a consanguinity or near affinity of a *being* impressed upon the part by on instantaneous imagination, and by a successive course of the years of its kernel : surely the more learned ought not to impute those things unto evil spirits, which, through their own weakness, they are ignorant of; for these things do on all sides occur in nature, the which, through our slenderness, we are not able to unfold; for to refer whatsoever gifts of God are in nature (because our dull capacity does not comprehend the same rightly) to the devil, shews both ignorance and rashness, especially when, as all demonstration of *causes* from a former thing or cause is banished from us, and especially from Aristotle, who was ignorant of all nature, and deprived of the good gifts which descends from the Father of Lights ; unto whom be all honour and glory.

Note. We may, by the aforesaid chapter, see the wonderful working power of the attractive or universal spirit, which can by no other means be so clearly demonstrated as by the sympathies in natural things, which are inherent throughout all nature ; and, upon this principle of sympathy and antipathy, we say is founded that spiritual power which tends to things and objects remote one from the other, *i. e.* a magnetic attraction, which does actually exist, as we shall clearly prove by experiment, where we fully shew the action and passion that is between natural spirits, by which means wonderful effects are produced which have ignorantly been attributed to divers superstitions, as *Sorcery, Inchantment, Nigromancy,* or *the Black Art,* &c.

CHAP.

C H A P. II.

IN the year 1639, a little book came forth, whose title was, ' The Sympathetical Powder of Edricius Mohynus, of Eburo,' whereby wounds are cured without application of the medicine unto the part afflicted, and without superstition; it being sifted by the sieve of the reasons of Galen and Aristotle; wherein it is Aristotetically, sufficiently, proved, whatsoever the title of it promises; but it hath neglected the *directive faculty*, or *virtue*, which may bring the virtues of the sympathetical powder, received in the bloody towel or napkin, unto the distant wound.

Truly, from a wound, the venal blood, or corrupt pus, or sanies, from an ulcer, being received in the towel, do receive, indeed, a balsam from a sanative or healing being; I say, from the power of the vitriol, a medicinal power connected and limited in the aforesaid mean; but the virtues of the balsam received are directed unto the wounded object, not indeed by an influential virtue of the stars, and much less do they fly forth of their own accord unto the object at a distance: therefore the ideas of him that applieth the sympathetical remedy are connected in the mean, and are made directresses of the balsam unto the object of his desire: even as we have above also minded by injections concerning ideas of the desire. Mohyns supposed that the power of sympathy depends upon the stars, because it is an imitator of influences: but I draw it out of a much nearer subject: to wit, out of directing ideas, begotten by their mother Charity, or a desire of goodwill: for, from hence does that sympathetic powder operate more successfully, being applied by the hand of one than another: therefore I have always observed the best process where the remedy is instituted by a desire of charity; but, that it doth succeed, with small success, if the operator be a careless or drunken person; and, from hence, I have more esteemed the stars of

the

the mind, in sympathetical remedies, than the stars of heaven : but that images, being conceived, are brought unto an object at a distance, a pregnant woman is an example of, because she is she who presently transfers all the ideas of her conception on her young, which dependeth no otherwise on the mother than from a communion of universal nourishment. Truly, seeing such a direction of desire is plainly natural, it is no wonder that the evil spirit doth require the ideas of the desires of his imps to be annexed unto a mean offered by him. Indeed, the ideas of the desire are after the manner of the influences of heaven cast into a proper object how locally remote soever ; that is, they are directed by the desire, especially pointing out an object for itself, even as the sight of the basilisk, or touch of the torpedo, is reflected on their willed object; for I have already shewn in its place, that the devil doth not attribute so much as any thing in the directions of things injected ; but that he hath need of a free, directing, and operative power or faculty. But I will not disgrace sympathetical remedies because the devil operates something about things injected into the body : for what have sympathetical remedies in common? Although Satan doth co-operate in injections by wicked natural means required from his bond slaves; for every thing shall be judged guilty, or good, from its ends and intents : and it is sufficient that sympathetical remedies do agree with things injected in *natural means*, or medicines.

C H A P. III.

OF THE MAGNETIC OR SYMPATHETIC UNGUENT, THE POWDER OF SYMPATHY, ARMARY UN-
GUENT, CURING OF WOUNDS, ECSTASIES, WITCHRAFT, MUMMIES, &C.

WE shall now show some remarkable operations that are effected by magnetism, and founded upon natural sympathy and antipathy, likewise how by these means some extraordinary cures may be performed.

Book II.   The

The goodness of the Creator every where extended, created every thing for the use of ungrateful man; neither did he admit any of the theologists, or divines, as assistants in council, how many or how great virtues he should infuse into things natural.　But there are those who venture to measure the wonderful works of God by their own sharpened and refined wit, whereby they deny God to have given such virtue to things; as though man (a worm) was able, by his narrow and limited capacity, to comprehend Omniscience; he therefore measures the minds of all men by his own, who think that cannot be done, which they cannot understand. *They* therefore can only develope the mysteries of nature, who being versed in the art of Cabala, Fire, and Magic, examined the properties of things, and draw, from darkness into light, the lurking powers of *Man, Animals, Vegetables, Minerals,* and *Stones ;* and, separating the crudities, dregs, poisons, heterogenities, that are the thorns implanted in virgin nature from the curse.　For an observer of nature sees daily she doth *distil, sublime, calcine, ferment, dissolve, coagulate, fix,* &c. therefore we who are the ministers of nature do separate, &c. finding out the causes and effects of every phænomena she produces.

Now, as magnetism is ordained for the use of man, and for the curing of the various disorders incident to human nature, we shall first touch upon the grand subject of magnetism, known to possess wonderful properties, and which are not only evident to every eye, but shew us sufficient grounds for our admitting the possibility and reality of magnetism in general.

The loadstone possesses an eminent medicinal faculty against many violent and implacable disorders.　Helmont says, that the back of the loadstone, as it repulses iron, so also it removes gout, swellings, rheum, &c. that is of the nature or quality of iron.　The iron attracting faculty, if it be joined to the mummy of a woman, and the back of the loadstone be put within her thigh, and the belly of the loadstone on her loins, it safely prevents a miscarriage, already threatened; but the belly of the loadstone applied within the thigh and the back to her loins, it doth wonderfully facilitate her delivery.

Likewise the wearing the loadstone eases and prevents the cramp, and such like disorders and pains..

Uldericus

Uldericus Balk, a dominican friar, published a book at Frankfort in the year 1611, concerning the lamp of life; in which we shall find (taken from Paracelsus) the true magnetical cure of many diseases, *viz.* the dropsy, gout, jaundice, &c. For if thou shalt enclose the warm blood of the sick in the shell and white of an egg, which is exposed to a nourishing warmth, and this blood, being mixed with a piece of flesh, thou shalt give to a hungry dog, the disorder departs from thee into the dog; no otherwise than the leprosy of Naaman passed over into Gehazi through the execration of the prophet.

If women, weaning their infants, shall milk out their milk upon hot burning coals, the breast soon dries.

If any one happens to commit nuisance at thy door, and thou wilt prevent that beastly trick in future, take the poker red-hot, and put it into the excrement, and, by magnetism, his posteriors shall become much scorched and inflamed.

Make a small table of the lightest, whitest, and basest kind of lead; and at one end put a piece of amber, and, three spans from it, lay a piece of green vitriol; this vitriol will soon lose its colour and acid: both which effects are found in the preparation of amber. The root of the Caroline thistle being plucked up when full of juice and virtue, and tempered with the mummy of a man, will exhaust the powers and natural strength out of a man, on whose shadow thou shalt stand, into thyself.

CHAP.

CHAP. IV.

OF THE ARMARY UNGUENT, OR WEAPON SALVE, &c.

THE principal ingredient in this confection, is the moss of a dead man's skull, which Van Helmont calls the excrescencies or superfluities of the stars. Now the moss growing on the skull of a dead man, seeing it has received its seed from the heavens, but its increase from the mummial marrow of the skull of man, or tower of the microcosm, has obtained excellent astral and magnetic powers beyond the common condition of vegetables, although herbs, as they are herbs, want not their own magnetism.

Now, the magnetism of this unguent draws out that strange disposition from the wound (which otherwise, by a disunion of the parts that held together, and by which, I say, strange disposition and foreign quality is produced) from whence it slips, not being overburdened or oppressed by any accident, suddenly grow together; and this is effected by the armary unguent, or weapon salve. From this it appears that the unguent, or weapon salve, its property is to heal suddenly and perfectly without pain, costs, peril, or loss of strength; hence it is manifest that the magnetical virtue is from God.

It is now seasonable to discover the immediate cause of magnetism in the unguent.

First of all, by the consent of mystical divines, we divide man into the external and internal man, assigning to both the powers of a certain mind, or intelligence: for so there doth a will belong to flesh and blood, which may not be either the will of man or the will of God; and the heavenly Father also reveals some things unto the more inward man, and some things flesh and blood reveals, that is, the outward and sensitive, or animal man. For, how could the service of idols, envy, &c. be rightly numbered among the works of the flesh, seeing they consist only in the imagination, if the flesh had not also its own imagination and elective will?

Furthermore, that there are miraculous ecstasies belonging to the more inward man, is beyond dispute. That there are also ecstasies in the animal man,

by

by reason of an intense, or heightend imagination, is, without doubt. Martin del Ris, an elder of the society of Jesus, in his Magical Disquisitions or Enquiries, makes mention of a certain young man in the city Insulis that was transported with so violent a desire of seeing his mother, that through the same intense desire, as if being rapt up by an ecstasy, he saw her perfectly, although many miles absent from thence; and, returning again to himself, being mindful of all that he had seen, gave many true signs of his true presence with his mother.

Now that desire arose from the more outward man, *viz.* from blood and sense, or flesh, is certain; for, otherwise, the soul being once dislodged, or loosened from the bonds of the body, cannot, except by miracle, be reunited to it; there is therefore in the blood a certain ecstatical or transporting power, which, if at any time shall be excited or stirred up by an ardent desire and most strong imagination, it is able to conduct the spirit of the more outward man even to some absent and far distant object, but then that power lies hid in the more outward man, as it were, in *potentia*, or by way of possibility; neither is it brought into act, unless it be roused up by the imagination, inflamed and agitated by a most fervent and violent desire.

CHAP. V.

OF THE IMAGINATIVE POWER AND THE MAGNETISM OF THE NATURAL SPIRITS, MUMMIAL ATTRACTION, SYMPATHIES OF ASTRAL SPIRITS, WITH THEIR BODIES, UPON WHICH THE WHOLE ART OF NECROMANCY IS FOUNDED.

MOREOVER, when as the blood is after some sort corrupted, then indeed all the powers thereof which, without a foregoing excitation of the imagination, were before in possibility, are of their own accord, drawn forth into action; for, through corruption of the grain, the seminal virtue, otherwise drowsy, and barren, breaks forth into act; because, that seeing the essences of things, and

their

their vital spirits, know not how to putrify by the dissolution of the inferior harmony, they sprung up as surviving afresh.   For, from thence it is that every occult property, the compact of their bodies being by foregoing digestion, (which we call putrifaction) now dissolved, comes forth free to hand, dispatched, and manifest for action.

Therefore when a wound, through the entrance of air, hath admitted of an adverse quality, from whence the blood forthwith swells with heat or rage in its lips, and otherwise becomes mattery, it happens, that the blood in the wound just made, by reason of the said foreign quality, doth now enter into the beginning of some kind of corruption (which blood being also then received on the weapon or splinter thereof, is besmeared with the magnetic unguent) the which entrance of corruption, mediating the ecstatical power lurking potentially in the blood, is brought forth into action; which power, because it is an exiled returner unto its own body, by reason of the hidden ecstasy; hence that blood bears an individual respect unto the blood of its whole body.   Then indeed the magnetic or attractive faculty is busied in operating in the unguent, and through the mediation of the ecstatical power (for so I call it for want of an etymology) sucks out the hurtful quality from the lips of the wound, and at length, through the mummial, balsamical, and attractive virtue, attained in the unguent, the magnetism is perfected.

So thou hast now the positive reason of the natural magnetism in the unguent, drawn from natural magic, whereunto the light of truth assents; saying, "where the treasure is there is the heart also."

For if the treasure be in heaven, then the heart, that is, the spirit of the internal man, is in God, who is the paradise, who alone is eternal life.

But if the treasure be fixed or laid up in frail and mortal things, then also the heart and spirit of the external man is in fading things; neither is there any cause of bringing in a mystical sense, by taking not the spirit, but the cogitation and naked desire, for the heart; for that would contain a frivolous thing, that wheresoever a man should place his treasure in his thought or cogitation, there his cogitation would be.

Also truth itself doth not interpret the present text mystically, and also by an example adjoined, shews a local and real presence of the eagles with the dead

carcass,

carcass, so also that the spirit of the inward man is locally in the kingdom of God in us, which is God himself; and that the heart or spirit of the animal or outward sensitive man is locally about its treasure.

What wonder is it, that the astral spirits of carnal or animal men should, as yet, after their funerals, shew themselves as in a bravery, wandering about their buried treasure, whereunto the whole of Necromancy (or art of divination by the calling of spirits) of the antients hath enslaved itself?

I say, therefore, that the internal man is an animal or living creature, making use of the reason and will of blood: but, in the mean time, not barely an animal, but moreover the image of God.

Logicians therefore may see how defectively they define a man from the power of rational discourse.   But of these things more elsewhere.

I will therefore adjoin the magnetism of eagles to carcasses; for neither are flying fowls endowed with such an acute smelling, that they can, with a mutual consent, go from Italy into Africa unto carcasses.

For neither is an odour so largely and widely spread; for the ample latitude of the interposed sea hinders it, and also a certain elementary property of consuming it; nor is there any ground that thou shouldest think these birds do perceive the dead carcasses at so far a distance, with their sight, especially if those birds shall lie southwards behind a mountain.

But what need is there to enforce the magnetism of fowls by many arguments, since God himself, who is the beginning and end of philosophy, doth expressly determine the same process to be of the heart and treasure, with these birds and the carcass, and so interchangeably between these and them?

For if the eagles were led to their food, the carcasses, with the same appetite whereby four-footed beasts are brought on to their pastures, certainly he had said, in one word, that living creatures flock to their food even as the heart of man to his treasure; which would contain a falsehood: for neither doth the heart of man proceed unto its treasure, that he may be filled therewith as living creatures do to their meat; and therefore the comparison of the heart of man and of the eagle lies not in the end for which they tend or incline to a desire, but in the manner of tendency; namely that they are allured and carried on by magnetism, really and locally.

Therefore

Therefore the spirit and will of the blood fetched out of the wound, having intruded itself into the ointment by the weapon being anointed therewith, do tend towards their treasure, that is, the rest of the blood as yet enjoying the life of the more inward man : but he saith by a peculiar testimony, that the eagle is drawn to the carcass, because she is called thereunto by an implanted and mummial spirit of the carcass, but not by the odour of the putrifying body : for indeed that animal, in assimilating, appropriates to himself only this mummial spirit : for from thence it is said of the eagle, in a peculiar manner, "my youth shall be renewed as the eagle's."

For truly the renewing of her youth proceeds from an essential extraction of the mummial spirit being well refined by a certain singular digestion proper to that fowl, and not from a bare eating of the flesh of the carcass ; otherwise dogs also and pies would be renewed, which is false.

Thou wilt say, that it is a reason far-fetched in behalf of magnetism ; but what wilt thou then infer hereupon ? If that which thou confesseth to be far remote for thy capacity of understanding, that shall also with thee be accounted to be fetched from far. Truly the book of Genesis avoucheth, that in the blood of all living creatures doth their soul exist.

For there are in the blood certain vital powers *, the which, as if they were soulified or enlivened, do demand revenge from Heaven, yea, and judicial punishment from earthly judges on the murderer ; which powers, seeing they cannot be denied to inhabit naturally in the blood, I see not why they can

---

* This singular property of the blood, which Helmont calls *Vital Powers*, is no less wonderful than true, having been myself a witness of this experiment while in South Wales. It was tried upon a body that was maliciously murdered, through occasion of a quarrel over-night at an alehouse. The fellow who was suspected of the murder appeared the next day in public seemingly unconcerned. The Coroner's Jury sat upon the body within twenty-four hours after this notable murder was committed ; when the suspected was suddenly taken into custody, and conveyed away to the same public-house where the inquisition was taken. After some debate, one Dr. Jones desired the suspected to be brought into the room ; which done, he desired the villain to lay his left hand under the wound, which was a deep gash on the neck, and another on the breast ; the villain plainly confessed his guilt by his trepidation ; but as soon as he lightly laid his finger on the body, the blood immediately ran, about six or seven drops, to the admiration of all present. If any one doubts the truth of this narrative, however learned and profound he may think himself, let him call personally upon me, and I will give him such reference, and that truly respectable and fair, as shall convince him of the fact. FRANCIS BARRETT.

reject

reject the magnetism of the blood, as accounting it among the ridiculous works of Satan.

This I will say more, to wit, that those who walk in their sleep, do, by no other guide than the spirit of the blood, that is, of the outward man, walk up and down, perform business, climb walls, and manage things that are otherwise impossible to those that are awake. I say, by a magical virtue, natural to the more outward man; that Saint Ambrose, although he was for distant in his body, yet was visibly present at the funeral solemnities of Saint Martin; yet was he spiritually present at those solemnities, in the visible spirit of the external man, and no otherwise : for inasmuch as in that ecstasy which is of the more internal man, many of the saints have seen many and absent things. This is done without time and place, through the superior powers of the soul being collected in unity, and by an intellectual vision, but not by a visible presence; otherwise the soul is not separated from the body, but in good earnest, or for altogether; neither is it re-connected thereunto, which re-connexion, notwithstanding, is otherwise natural or familiar to the spirit of the more outward man.

It is not sufficient in so great a paradox, to have once, or by one single reason, touched at the matter; it is to be further propagated, and we must explain how a magnetical attraction happens also between inanimate things, by a certain perceivance or feeling; not indeed animal or sensitive, but natural.

Which thing, that it may be the more seriously done, it behoves us first to shew what Satan can, of his own power, contribute to, and after what manner he can co-operate in the merely wicked and impious actions of witches : for, from thence it will appear unto what cause every effect may be attributed.

In the next place, what that spiritual power may be which tends to a far remote object; or what may be the action, passion, and skirmishing between natural spirits, or what may be the superiority of man as to other inferior creatures; and, by consequence, why indeed our unguent, being compounded of human mummies, do thoroughly cure horses also. We will explain the matter in the following chapter.

Book II. CHAP.

C H A P.   VI.

OF WITCHCRAFT.

LET a witch therefore be granted, who can strongly torment an absent man by an image of wax, by imprecation or cursing, by enchantment, or also by a foregoing touch alone, (for here we speak nothing of Sorceries, because they are those which kill only by poison, inasmuch as every common apothecary can imitate those things) that this act is diabolical, no man doubts: however, it is profitable to discern how much Satan and how much the witch can contribute hereunto.

The First Supposition.

First of all, thou shalt take notice, that Satan is the sworn and irreconcileable enemy of man, and to be so accounted by all, unless any one had rather have him to be his friend; and therefore he most readily procures whatsoever mischief he is able to cause or wish unto us, and that without doubt and neglect.

The Second Supposition.

And then although he be an enemy to witches themselves, forasmuch as he is also a most malicious enemy to all mankind in general; yet, in regard they are his bond-slaves, and those of his kingdom, he never, unless against his will betrays them, or discovers them to judges, &c.

From the former supposition I conclude, that if Satan were able of himself to kill a man who is guilty of deadly sin, he would never delay it; but he doth not kill him, therefore he cannot.

Notwithstanding, the witch doth oftentimes kill; hence also she can kill the same man, no otherwise than as a privy murderer at the liberty of his own will slays any one with a sword.

There

There is therefore a certain power of the witch in this action, which belongs not to Satan, and consequently Satan is not the principal efficient and executor of that murder ; for otherwise if he were the executioner thereof, he would in nowise stand in need of the witch as his assistant ; but he alone had soon taken the greatest part of men out of the way.

Surely most miserable were the conditions of mortals who should be subject to such a tyrant, and stand liable to his commands ; we have too faithful a God, than that he should subject the work of his own hands to the arbitrary dominion of Satan.

Therefore in this act, there is a certain power plainly proper and natural to the witch which belongs not to Satan.

Moreover, of what nature, extent, and quality that power may be, we must more exactly sift out.

In the first place, it is manifest that it is no corporeal strength of the male sex ; for neither doth there concur any strong touching of the extreme parts of the body, and witches are for the most part feeble, impotent, and malicious old women, therefore there must needs be some other power, far superior to a corporeal attempt, yet natural to man.

This power therefore was to be seated in that part wherein we most nearly resemble the image of God ; and although all things do also, after some sort, represent that venerable image, yet because man doth most elegantly, properly, and nearly do that, therefore the image of God in man doth far outshine, bear rule over, and command the images of God in all other creatures ; for, peradventure, by this prerogative, all things are put under his feet.

Wherefore if God act, *per nutum*, or by a beck, namely by his word, so ought man to act some things only by his beck or will, if he ought to be called his true image : for neither is that new, is that troublesome, is that proper to God alone : for Satan, the most vile abject of creatures, doth also locally move bodies *per nutum*, or by his beck alone, seeing he hath not extremities or corporeal organs, whereby to touch, move, or also to snatch a new body to himself.

That

That privilege therefore ought no less to belong to the inward man, as he is a spirit, if he ought to represent the image of God, and that indeed not an idle one; if we call this faculty magical, and thou being badly instructed, art terrified at this word, thou mayest, for me, call it a spiritual strength or efficacy: for, truly, we are nothing solicitous about names. I always, as immediately as I can, cast an eye upon the thing itself.

That magical power, therefore, is in the inward man, whether thou, by this etymology, or true word, understandest the soul or the vital spirit thereof, it is now indifferent to us; since there is a certain proportion of the internal man towards the external in all things, glowing or growing after its own manner, which is an appropriated disposition, and proportioned property.

Wherefore the power or faculty must needs be dispersed throughout the whole man; in the soul, indeed, more vigorous, but in the flesh and blood far more remiss.

C H A P. VII.

OF THE VITAL SPIRIT, &c.

THE vital spirit in the flesh and blood performs the office of the soul; that is, it is the same spirit in the outward man, which, in the seed, forms the whole figure, that magnificent structure and perfect delineation of man, and which hath known the ends of things to be done, because it contains them; and the which as president accompanies the new framed young, even unto the period of its life; and the which, although it depart therewith, some smacks or small quantity, at least, thereof remains in a carcass slain by violence, being as it were most exactly co-fermented with the same. But, from a dead carcass that was extinct of its own accord, and from nature failing, as well the implanted as inflowing spirit passed forth at once.

For

For which reason, physicians divide this spirit into the implanted or mummial, and inflowing or acquired spirit, which departs; to wit, with the former life and this influxing spirit they afterwards subdivide into the natural, vital, and animal spirit; but, we likewise, do here comprehend them all at once in one single word.

The soul therefore being wholly a spirit could never move or stir up the vital spirit, (being indeed corporeal), much less flesh and bones, unless a certain natural power, yet magical and spiritual, did descend from the soul into the spirit and body.

After what sort, I pray, could the corporeal spirit obey the commands of the soul, unless there should be a command from her for moving of the spirit, and afterwards the body?

But against this magical motive faculty thou will forthwith object, that that power is limited within her composed body, and her own natural inn : therefore although we call this soul a magicianness, yet it shall be only a wresting and abuse of the name ; for truly the true and superstitious magic draws not its foundation from the soul ; seeing this same soul is not able to move, alter, or exite any thing out of its own body.

I answer, that this power, and that natural magic of the soul which she exerciseth not of herself, by virtue of the image of God, doth now lie hid as obscure in man, and as it were lie asleep since the fall or corruption of Adam, and stands in need or stirring up; all which particulars we shall anon in their proper place prove; which same power, how drowsy and as it were drunk soever, it otherwise remains daily in us, yet it is sufficient to perform its offices in its own body.

CHAP.

C H A P. VIII.

OF THE MAGICAL POWER, &C.

THEREFORE the knowledge and power magical, and that faculty in man which acteth only *per nutum*, sleeps since the knowledge of the apple was eaten ; and as long as this knowledge (which is of the flesh and blood, gross and material, belonging to the external man and darkness) flourishes, the more noble magical power is lying dormant.

But because in sleep this outward or sensual knowledge is sometimes dormant, hence it is that our dreams are sometimes prophetical, and God himself is therefore nearer unto man in dreams, through that effect, *viz.* when the more inward magic of the soul being uninterrupted by the flesh, diffuses itself on every side into the understanding ; even as when it sinks itself into the inferior powers thereof it safely leads those who walk in their sleep by moving or conducting them, whither those that were awake could not surmount or climb.

Therefore we establish this point, *viz.* that there is inherent in the soul a certain magical virtue given her by God, naturally proper and belonging to her, in asmuch as we are his image and engravement ; and in this respect she acts also in a peculiar manner, *i. e.* spiritually on an object at a distance, and that more powerfully than by any corporeal assistance ; for seeing the soul is the principal part of the body, therefore all action belonging to her is spiritual, magical, and of the greatest validity.

Which power man is able, by the Art of the Cabala, to excite in himself at his own pleasure, and these, as we have before said, are called Adepts ; who are governed by the Spirit of God.

Thus we have endeavoured to shew that man predominates over all other creatures that are corporeal, and that by his magical faculty he is able to subdue the magical virtues of all other things ; which predominance of man, or the

soul's

soul's natural magic, some have ignorantly attributed solely to *verses*, *charms*, *signs*, *characters*, &c. by which hierarchy or holy dominion inherent in man, those effects, whatever they may be, are wrought, which some (who but too corporeally philosophize) have attributed to the dominion of Satan.

High and sacred is the force of the microcosmical spirit, which, as is evident in pregnant women, stamps upon the young the image and properties of a thing desired, as we have before instanced in a cherry, which, without the trunk of a tree, brings forth a true cherry, that is flesh and blood, enobled with the properties and power of the more inward or real cherry, by the conception of the imagination alone; from whence are two necessary consequences.

First, that all the spirits, and as it were the essences of all things, lie hid in us, and are born and brought forth only by the working, power, and phantasy of the microcosm.

The second is, that the soul, in conceiving, generates a certain idea of the thing conceived; the which, as it before lay hid unknown, like fire in a flint, so by the stirring up of the phantasy there is produced a certain real idea, which is not a naked quality, but something like a substance, hanging in suspense between a body and a spirit, that is the soul.

That middle being is so spiritual, that it is not plainly exempted from a corporeal condition, since the actions of the soul are limited on the body, and the inferior orders of faculties depending upon it, nor yet so corporeal that it may be inclosed by dimensions, the which we have also related to be only proper to a seminal being. This ideal entity, therefore, when it falls out of the invisible and intellectual world of the microcosm, it puts on a body, and then it is first inclosed by the limitation of place and numbers.

The object of the understanding is in itself a naked and pure essence, not an accident, by the consent of practical, that is, mystical divines; therefore this Proteus or transferable essence, the understanding doth, as it were, put on and clothe itself, with this conceived essence.

But because every body, whether external or internal, hath its making in its own proper image, the understanding knows or discerns not, the will loves and wills not, the memory recollects not, but by images or likenesses : the under-

standing

standing therefore puts on this same image of its object; and because the soul is the pure simple form of the body, which turns itself about to every member, therefore the acting understanding cannot have two images at once, but first one and then the other. He, who is wholly the life, created all things and hath said, nothing is to be expected as dead out of his hand. Likewise nothing can come to our view wherein himself is not clearly apparent or present; for it is said, "the spirit of the Lord hath filled the whole globe of the earth:" and, again, "that he containeth or comprehendeth all things," therefore there is nothing in being, no creature but what possesses a certain degree of divine fire and life, yet lying dormant or unexcited, till stirred up by the art, power, and operation of man.

C H A P. IX.

OF THE EXCITING OR STIRRING UP THE MAGICAL VIRTUE.

EVERY magical virtue therefore stands in need of an excitement, by which a certain spiritual vapour is stirred up, by reason whereof the phantasy which profoundly sleeps is awakened, and there begins an action of the corporeal spirit, as a medium, which is that of Magnetism, and is excited by a foregoing touch.

There is a magical virtue, being as it were abstracted from the body, which is wrought by the stirring up of the power of the soul, from whence there are made most potent procreations, and most famous impressions, and strong effects, so that nature is on every side a magicianness, and acts by her own phantasy; and by how much the more spiritual her phantasy is, so much the more powerful it is, therefore the denomination of magic is truly proportionable or concordant.

Now

Now the highest sort of magic is that which is stirred up from an intellectual conception, and indeed that of the inward man is only to be excited by the Holy Spirit, and by his gift the Cabala ; but that of the external man is stirred up by a strong imagination, by a daily and heightened speculation, and, in witches, by the devil.

But the magical virtue of the exhaled spirituous vapour, or subtil spirits sent from the body, which before lay *in potentia*, or by way of possibility only, is either excited by a more strong imagination, the magician making use of the blood as a medium, and establishing his kindled entity thereon, or by the ascending phantasy of the weapon salve, the exciteress of the property lying in the blood; else by a foregoing appointment or disposition of the blood unto corruption, *viz.* whereby the elements are disposed unto a separation, and the essences (which cannot putrify) and the essential phantasies, which lay hid in the properties come forth into action.

The phantasy therefore, of any subject whatsoever has obtained a strong appetite to the spirit of another thing, for the moving of some certain thing in place, for the attracting, repelling, or expulsion thereof ; and there and not elsewhere we acknowledge magnetism as the natural magical endowment of that thing firmly planted in it by God.

There is therefore a certain formal property separated from sympathetical and abstruse qualities ; because the motive phantasy of these qualities do not directly fly unto a local motion, but only to an alternative motion of the object. Now it is sufficient that (if a man happens to receive many wounds in his body) blood be had only from one of these wounds, and from this one the rest are cured also, because that blood keeps a concordant harmony with the spirit of the whole, and draws forth from the same the offensive quality communicated, not only to the lips of the wound, but to the whole man, for from one wound only the whole man is liable to grow feverish.

Therefore the outchased blood being received on the weapon is introduced into the magnetic unguent.

For then the phantasy of the blood, being otherwise as yet drowsy and slow to action, being stirred up by the virtue of the magnetic unguent, and there finding

Book II.   the

the balsamic virtue of it, desires the quality induced into it, to be bestowed on itself throughout, and from thence by a spiritual magnetism to draw out all the strange tincture of the wound, which, seeing it cannot fitly enough effect by itself, it implores the aid of the *moss, blood, fat,* and *mummy*, which are conjoined together into such a balsam, which not but by its own phantasy becomes also medicinal, magnetical, and is also a tractor of all the strange qualities out of the body, whose fresh blood, abounding with spirit, is carried unto it, whether it shall be that of a man or any other living creature. The phantasy therefore is a returner, or reducible and ecstatical, from part of the blood that is fresh and newly brought unto the unguent; but the magnetic attraction began in the blood is perfected by the medicinal virtue of the unguent; not that the unguent draws the infirmity of the wound unto itself, but it alters the blood newly brought unto it, in its spirit, and makes it medicinal, and stirs up the power thereof : from thence it contracts a certain medicinal virtue, which returns unto its whole body to correct the spirit of the blood throughout the whole man. Now, to manifest a great mystery, *viz.* to shew that in man there is placed a great efficacy whereby he may be able only by his beck, (as we before mentioned) nod or phantasy, to act out of himself, and to imprint a virtue, a certain influence which afterwards perseveres, or constantly subsists by itself, and acts upon objects at a very great distance ; by which only mystery, those things which we have spoken (relative to ideal entity conveyed in a spiritual fewel, and departing far from home to execute its offices, concerning the magnetism of all things begotten in the imagination of man, as in that which is proper to every thing, and also concerning the magical superiority of men over all other bodies,) will plainly and conspicuously appear.

CHAP.

C H A P. X.

OF THE MAGICAL VIRTUE OF THE SOUL, AND THE MEDIUMS BY WHICH IT ACTS.

SOMETHING more we will add, before we dismiss the present subject, which is that if a nail, dart, knife, or sword, or any other iron instrument be thrust into the heart of a horse, it will bind and withhold the spirit of a witch, and conjoin it with the mummial spirit of the horse, whereby they may be burnt in the fire together, and by that the witch is tormented, as by a sting or burning, by which means she may be known so that she who is offensive to God, and destructive to mortal men, may be taken away from society according to the law of God " thou shalt not suffer a witch to live ; " for if the work be limited to any outward object, that work the magical soul never attempts without a medium or mean : therefore it makes use of the nail, or sword, or knife, or any other thing as aforesaid.

Now this being proved, that man hath a power of acting, *per nutum*, or by his nod, or of moving any object remotely placed ; it has also been sufficiently confirmed by the same natural example, that this efficacy was also given unto man by God.

And as every magical faculty lies dormant, and has need of excitement, or stirring up ; which is always true, if the object whereon it is to act is not nearly disposed, if its internal phantasy doth not wholly confirm to the impression of the agent, or also if the patient be equal in strength, or superior to the agent therein.

But, on the contrary, where the object is plainly and nearly disposed, as steel is, for the receiving of magnetism, then the patient without much stirring up, the alone phantasy of the more outward man being drawn out to the work and bound up to any suitable mean, yields to the magnetism.

Therefore we repeat, the magician must always make use of a medium ; for then the words or forms of sacraments do always operate, because from

the

the work performed. But the reason why exorcisms, conjurations, charms, incantations, &c. do sometimes fail of their desired effect, is because the unexcited mind, or spirit of the exorcist, renders the words dull or in-effectual.

Therefore no man can be a happy or successful magician, but him who knows how to stir up the magical virtue of his soul, or can do it practically without science.

And there can be no nearer medium of magnetism, than human blood with human blood.

And no sympathetic remedies, magnetical or attractive, but from the idea or phantasy of the operator impressing upon it a virtue and efficacy from the excited power in his own soul.

And now to bring our Magnetic Treatise to a total conclusion, we have to say, that whoever, through ignorance or obstinacy, will say there is no validity or reason, or reality in the science of magnetism, proves himself unworthy the sacred name of philosopher, because he condemns what he knows nothing at all about.

For those who will give themselves the leisure to examine the truth of those things which we have taught, will not find their expectation deceived, therefore will not condemn.

But whoever should be so superstitious as to attribute a natural effect so created by God, and bestowed on the creature, unto the power and craft of the devil, he filches the honour due to the Omnipotent Creator, and reproach-fully applies the same unto Satan ; the which (under favour) will be found to be express idolatry and blasphemy.

" There are three" (as says the Scripture) "who bear record in heaven ; the Father, the Word, and the Holy Spirit ; and these three are only one."

There are three that bear record on earth ; the *blood*, the *spirit*, and the *water ;* and these three are only *one.*

We therefore, who have the like humanity, contain blood and spirit of a co-like unity ; and the action of the blood is merely spiritual. Therefore, in

Genesis,

Genesis, it is not called by the etymology of *blood*, but is made remarkable by the name of a *red spirit*.

Therefore, let those who would attain knowledge in these things, and be perfect in what we have set before them, constantly meditate and desire that the First Cause and Archetype of all things would graciously and mercifully illuminate their minds ; without which, they grope but in darkness and uncertainty, and are subject to the delusions of impure spirits and devils, who are only to be put to flight by putting on the whole armour of God, in whom we all *live, move, breathe*, and have our being.

END OF MAGNETISM.

THE CABALA;

OR, THE

SECRET MYSTERIES

OF

CEREMONIAL MAGIC

ILLUSTRATED.

SHEWING

THE ART OF CALCULATING BY DIVINE NAMES;

The Rule, Order, and Government of

ANGELS, INTELLIGENCES, AND BLESSED SPIRITS;

Holy Seals, Pentacles, Tales of the Cabala, Divine Numbers, Characters and Letters;
Of Miracles, Prophecy, Dreams, &c. &c. &c.

Embellished and beautified with a vast Number of

RARE FIGURES, PENTACLES, CHARACTERS, &c. &c. &c.

Used in the

CABALISTIC ART.

By *FRANCIS BARRETT,*

STUDENT OF CHEMISTRY, NATURAL AND OCCULT PHILOSOPHY, THE CABALA, &C.

CABALISTICAL MAGIC.

CHAP. I.

OF THE CABALA, &C.

WE shall now turn our pen to the explaining of the high and mysterious secrets of the Cabala, by which only we can know the truth; and likewise how to prepare our mind and spirit for the contemplation of the greatest and best part of magic, which we call intellectual and divine, because it chiefly takes God and the good spirits for its object; and as the cabalistic art opens many and the chiefest mysteries and secrets of ceremonial magic.

But in respect of explaining or publishing those few secrets in the Cabala, which are amongst a few wise men, and communicated by word of mouth only, I hope the student will pardon me if I pass over these in silence, because we are not permitted to divulge some certain things; but this we shall do; we will open all those secrets which are necessary to be known; and by the close reading of which, you shall find out, of your own head, to be both profitable and delightful.

Therefore, all we solicit is, that those who perceive those secrets should keep them together as secrets, and not expose or babble them to the unworthy; but reveal them only to faithful, discreet, and chosen friends. And we would caution you in this beginning, that every magical experiment flies from the public, seeking to be hid, is strengthened and confirmed by silence, but is destroyed by publication; never does any complete effect follow after: likewise all the virtue of thy works will suffer detriment when poured into weak, prating, and incredulous minds; therefore, if thou would be a magician,

cian, and gain fruit from this art, to be secret, and to manifest to none, either thy *work*, or *place*, or *time*, nor thy *desire*, or *will*, except it be to a master or partner, or companion, who should likewise be faithful, discreet, silent, and dignified by nature and education ; seeing that even the prating of a companion, his unbelief, doubting, questioning, and, lastly, unworthiness, hinders and disturbs the effect in every operation.

CHAP. II.

WHAT DIGNITY AND PREPARATION IS ESSENTIALLY NECESSARY TO HIM WHO WOULD BECOME A TRUE MAGICIAN.

IT is fit that we who endeavour to attain so great a height should first study two things : *viz*. First, how we should leave vain and carnal affections, frail sense and material passions ; Secondly, by what ways and means we may ascend to an intellect pure, and joined with the powers of the celestials, without which we shall never happily ascend to the scrutiny of secret things, and to the power of working wonderful effects, *&c*. Now, if thou art a man perfect in thy understanding, and constantly meditating upon what we have in this book written, and without doubting, believeth, thou shalt be able, by praying, consecrating, deprecating, invocating, *&c*. to attract spiritual and celestial gifts, and to imprint them on whatever things thou shalt please ; and by it to vivify every magical work.

CHAP.

CHAP. III.

THAT THE KNOWLEDGE OF THE TRUE GOD IS NECESSARY FOR A MAGICIAN.

SEEING that the being and operation of all things depend on the Most High God, Creator of all things, and from thence on the other divine powers, to whom also is granted a power of fashioning and creating, not principally indeed, but instrumentally, by virtue of the First Great Creator, (for the beginning of every thing is the first cause; but what is produced by the second cause, is much more produced by the first, which is the producer of the second cause, which therefore we call secondaries.)   It is necessary, therefore, that every magician should know that very God, which is the first cause and creator of all things, and likewise the other divine powers, (which we call the second causes,) and not to be ignorant of them, and likewise what holy rites, ceremonies, &c. are conformable to them; but, above all, we are to worship in spirit and truth, and place our firm dependance upon that one only God who is the author and promoter of all good things, the Father of all, most bountiful and wise; the sacred light of justice, and the absolute and sole perfection of all nature, and the contriver and wisdom thereof.

CHAP. IV.

OF DIVINE EMANATIONS, AND TEN SEPHIROTHS, AND TEN MOST SACRED NAMES OF GOD WHICH RULE THEM, AND THE INTERPRETATION OF THEM.

GOD himself, although he is trinity in persons, yet he is but one only simple essence; yet we doubt not but that there are in him many divine powers, which emanate or flow from him.

The

The Cabalists most learned in divine things have received the ten principal names of God, as certain divine powers, or, as it were, members of God; which, by ten numerations, which we call Sephiroth, as it were vestiments, instruments, or exemplars of the Archetype, have an influence upon all created things, from the highest to the lowest; yet by a certain order: for first and immediately they have influence upon the nine orders of angels and quire of blessed souls, and by them into the celestial spheres, planets and men; by the which Sephiroth every thing receiveth power and virtue.

The first of these is the name *Eheia*, the name of the divine essence; his numeration is called Cether, which is interpreted a crown or diadem, and signifies the most simple essence of the divinity; and it is called that which the eye seeth not; and is attributed to God the Father, and hath its influence by the order of seraphims, or Hajoth Hakados, that is, creatures of holiness; and then by the *primum mobile*, it bestows the gift of being upon all things, and filleth the whole universe, both through the circumference and center; whose particular intelligence is called Merattron, that is the prince of faces, whose duty it is to bring others to the face of the Prince; and by him the Lord spake to Moses.

The second name is Jod, or Tetragrammaton joined with Jod; his numeration is Hochma, that is, wisdom, and signifies the divinity full of ideas, and the First Begotten; and is attributed to the Son, and has its influence by the order of cherubins, or that the Hebrews call Orphanim, *i. e.* forms or wheels; and from thence into the starry heavens, where he frames so many figures as he hath ideas in himself, and distinguishes the very chaos of the creatures, by a particular intelligence called Raziel, who was the ruler of *Adam*.

The third name is called Tetragrammaton Elohim; his numeration is named *Prina*, *viz*. providence and understanding; and signifies remissness, quietness, the jubilee, penitential conversion, a great trumpet, redemption of the world, and the life of the world to come: it is attributed to the Holy Spirit, and hath his influence by the order of thrones, or which the Hebrews call *Abalim*, that is great angels, mighty and strong; and from thence, by the sphere of *Saturn*, administers form to the unsettled matter, whose particular

cular intelligence is Zaphkiel, the ruler of Noah, and another intelligence named Jophiel, the ruler of Sem ; and these are the three supreme and highest numerations, as it were, seats of the divine persons, by whose command all things are made; but are executed by the other seven, which are therefore called numerations framing.

The fourth name is El, whose numeration is *Hesed*, which signifies clemency or goodness; likewise grace, mercy, piety, magnificence, the scepter, and right-hand; and hath its influx by the order of dominations, which the Hebrews called *Hasmalim ;* and so through the sphere of Jupiter fashions the images of bodies, bestowing clemency and pacifying justice on all : his particular intelligence is *Zadkiel*, the ruler of Abraham.

The fifth name is Elohim Gibor, that is, the mighty God, punishing the sins of the wicked; and his numeration is called Gebusach, which is to say, power, gravity, fortitude, security, judgment, punishing by slaughter and war ; and it is applied to the tribunal of God, the girdle, the sword, the left hand of God : it is also called Pachad, which is fear; and hath his influence through the order of powers, which the Hebrews call Seraphim, and from thence through the sphere of Mars, to whom belongs fortitude, war, and affliction.   It draweth forth the elements ; and his particular intelligence is *Camael*, the ruler of Samson.

The sixth name is *Eloha*, or a name of four letters joined with *Vaudahat;* his numeration is Tiphereth, that is, apparel, beauty, glory, pleasure, and signifies the tree of life, and hath his influence through the order of virtues, which the Hebrews call *Malachim*, that is, angels, into the sphere of the sun, giving brightness and life to it, and from thence producing metals ; his particular intelligence is *Raphael*, who was the ruler of *Isaac* and *Toby* the younger, and the angel *Peliel*, the Ruler of Jacob.

The seventh name is *Tetragrammaton Sabaoth*, or *Adonai Sabaoth*, that is, the God of Hosts ; and his numeration is *Nezah*, that is, triumph and victory : the right column is applied to it, and it signifies the justice and eternity of a revenging God ; it hath its influence through the orders of principalities, whom the Hebrews call *Elohim, i. e.* Gods, into the sphere of *Venus*, gives zeal and
love

love of righteousness, and produces vegetables; his intelligence is *Haniel*, and the angel *Cerviel*, the ruler of David.

The eighth is called also Elohim Sabaoth, which is likewise the God of Hosts, not of war and justice, but of piety and agreement, for this name signifies both, and precedeth his army; the numeration of this is called *Hod*, which is, praise, confession, honour and fame; the left column is attributed to it; it hath his influence through the order of the archangels, which the Hebrews call Ben Elohim, that is, the sons of God, into the sphere of Mercury, and gives elegancy, and consonancy of speech, and produces living creatures; his intelligence is Michael, who was the ruler of Solomon.

The ninth name is called *Sadai*, that is, Omnipotent, satisfying all, and *Elhai*, which is the Living God; his numeration is Jesod, that is, foundation, and signifies a good understanding, a covenant, redemption and rest; and hath his influence through the order of angels, whom the Hebrews name Cherubim, into the sphere of the moon causing the increase and decrease of all things, and provideth for the genii and keepers of men, and distributeth them; his intelligence is *Gabriel*, who was the keeper of *Joseph*, *Joshua*, and *Daniel*.

The tenth name is *Adonai Melech*, that is, lord and king; his numeration is *Malchuth*, that is, kingdom and empire, and signifies a church, the temple of God, and a gate; and hath his influence through the order of *Animastic*, *viz.* of *blessed souls*, which, by the Hebrews, is called Issim, that is, nobles, lords, and princes; they are inferior to the *hierarchies*, and have their influences on the sons of men, and give knowledge and the wonderful understanding of things, also industry and prophecy; and the soul of the Messiah is president amongst them, or the intelligence Merattron, which is called the first creature, or the soul of the world, who was the ruler of Moses.

                                                        CHAP.

C H A P. V.

OF THE POWER AND VIRTUE OF THE DIVINE NAMES.

GOD himself, though he be one only essence, yet hath divers names, which expound not his divers essences or deities; but certain properties flowing from him; by which names he pours down upon us, and all his creatures, many benefits; ten of those names we have above described. The Cabalists, from a certain text of Exodus, derive seventy-two names, both of the angels and of God, which they call the name of seventy-two letters and Schemhamphores, that is, the expository. From these therefore, besides those which we have reckoned up before, is the name of the divine essence, *Eheia*, אהיה, which Plato translates ὤν, from hence they call God τοὄν, others ὀων, that is, the Being. *Hu*, הוא, is another name revealed to Esay, signifying the abyss of the godhead, which the Greeks translate ταυτὸν, the Latins, himself the same. *Esch*, אש, is another name received from Moses, which soundeth fire, and is the name of God; *Na*, נא, is to be invocated in perturbations and troubles. There is also the name Ja, יה, and the name Elion, עליון, and the name *Macom*, מוקם, the name *Caphu*, בפכ, the name *Innon*, יונ, and the name *Emeth*, אמה, which is interpreted truth, and is the seal of God; and there are two other names, *Zur*, צור, and *Aben*, אבן, both of these signify a solid work, and one of them expresseth the Father with the Son; and many names we have placed in the scale of numbers; and many names of God and the angels, are extracted out of the Holy Scriptures by our Cabala, and the Notarian and Gimetrian arts, where many words retracted by certain of their letters, make up one name; or one name dispersed by each of its letters, signifies or renders more. Sometimes they are gathered from the heads of words, as the name *Agla*, אגלא, from this verse of the Holy Scripture, *viz.* אתהגיבר לעולםארכי, that is, the Mighty God for ever. In like manner the name *Iaia*, יאיא, from this verse, *viz.* הוהאלהינו יהוהאהר, that is, God our God is one God; in like manner the name *Java*, יאוא, from

this

this verse, יהי אור ויהיאור, that is, let there be light and there was light : in like manner the name *Ararita*, אראריתא, from this verse, אהרותז ראש ייהורו תמורהזואהר אהר ראש, that is, one principal of his unity, one beginning of his individuality, his vicissitude is one thing ; and this name *Hacaba*, הקבא, is extracted from this verse, יהקרושכברהוא, the holy and blessed One ; in like manner this name, *Jesu*, ישו, is found in the heads of these two verses, *viz.*, יביאשלוהולו, that is until the Messiah shall come ; and the other verse, ינון שמוית, that is, his name abides till the end. Thus also is the name *Amen*, אמנ, extracted from this verse, ארניטלר נאטן, that is, *the Lord is the faithful King.* Sometimes these names are extracted from the ends of words, as the same Amen from this verse, לאב והרשעים, that is, *the wicked not so ;* but the letters are transposed : so, by the final letters of this verse, לימה שמזמח, that is, *to me what ?* or *what is his name ?* is found the name Tetragrammaton : in all these a letter is put for a word, and a letter extracted from a word, either from the beginning, end, or where you please ; and sometimes these names are extracted from all the letters, one by one, even as those seven-two names of God are extracted from those three verses of Exodus, beginning from these three words, יוסעו ידאו יט, the first and the last verses being written from the right to the left ; but the middle contrariwise, from the left to the right, as we shall shew hereafter ; and so sometimes a word is extracted from a word, or a name from a name, by the transposition of letters, as *Messia*, משיה, from *Ismah*, ישמה, and *Michael* from *Malachi*, מלאבי ; but sometimes by changing the alphabet, which the Cabalists call *Ziruph*, צירוף ; so from the name *Tetragrammaton*, יהוה, are drawn forth טצפע, *Maz-Paz*, בוזו, *Kuzu.* Sometimes, by reason of the equality of the numbers, names are changed, as *Merattron*, מטטרון, *pro Sadai* שרי, for both of them make three hundred and fourteen ; so *Jiai*, ייא, and *El*, אל, are equal in number, for both make thirty-one ; and these are the hidden secrets, concerning which it is most difficult to judge, or to deliver a perfect science ; neither can they be understood or taught in any other language but the Hebrew. Therefore, these sacred words have not their power in magical operations from themselves, as they are words, but from the occult divine powers working by them in the mind of those who by faith adhere to them.

We

The Cabala.
Holy Sigils of the
Names of God.

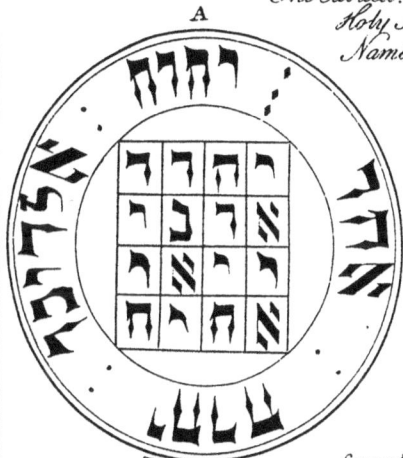

A

B

The front part

The hinder part

Sacred Pentacles

This Sigil against all dangers
& mischiefs of evil Spirits & Men

The fore part   צמרבה

The hinder part   בווור

This Seal is used as a preservative
against all casualties, dangers &
mischief, being worn engraven on pure
Gold it secures the bearer from all evils.

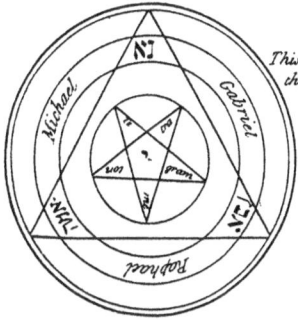

This is to be engraven on
the other side.

Michael   Gabriel

Raphael

Pub by Lackington Allen & Co

We will here deliver unto thee a sacred seal, efficacious against any disease of man, or any griefs whatsoever, in whose fore-side are the four-squared names of God, so subordinate to one another in a square, that, from the highest to the lowest, those most holy names or seals of the godhead do arise, whose intention is inscribed in the circumference; but on the backside is inscribed the *seven-lettered name Araritha,* and his interpretation is written about, *viz.* the verse from which it is extracted, even as you may see in the annexed plate, where A represents the former part, B the hinder; but all this must be done in most pure gold, or virgin parchment, pure, clean, and unspotted; also with ink made of the smoke of consecrated wax-lights, or incense and holy water. The operator must be purified and cleansed, and have an infallible hope, a constant faith, and have his mind lifted up to the Most High God, if he would surely obtain this divine power.

Now, against the depredations of evil spirits and men, and what dangers soever, either of journies, waters, enemies, arms, *&c.* in the same manner as is above said, these characters on the one side בראו, and these on the other עשכה, which are the beginnings and ends of the five first verses of *Genesis,* and representation of the creation of the world; and, by this ligature, they say that a man shall be free from all mischiefs, if that he firmly believes in God, the Creator of all things.

Now these being done on a small plate of gold, as before described, (will be found to have the effect above mentioned); the figure of which you may likewise see in the annexed plate, fig. C and D, where C shows the former part, and B the hinder.

Now let no one distrust or wonder, that sacred words and divine names applied outwardly, can effect wonderful things, seeing, by them, the Almighty created the heavens and the earth; for there is no name of God amongst us (according to Moses the Egyptian) which is not taken from his works, besides the name Tetragrammaton, which is holy, signifying the substance of the Creator in a pure signification.

Book II. CHAP.

CHAP. VI.

OF INTELLIGENCES AND SPIRITS, AND OF THE THREE-FOLD KIND OF THEM, AND OF THEIR
DIFFERENT NAMES, AND OF INFERNAL AND SUBTERRANEAL SPIRITS.

NOW, consequently, we must discourse of intelligences, spirits, and angels. An intelligence is an intelligible substance, free from all gross and putrifying mass of a body, immortal, insensible, assisting all, having influence over all; and the nature of all intelligences, spirits, and angels is the same. But I call angels here, not those whom we usually call devils, but spirits so called from the propriety of the word, as it were, knowing, understanding, and wise. But of these, according to the tradition of magicians, there are three kinds; the first of which we call super-celestial, and minds altogether separated from a body, and, as it were, intellectual spheres worshipping one only God, as it were, their most firm and stable unity or centre. Wherefore they even call them Gods, by reason of a certain participation of the Divinity, for they are always full of God. These are only about God, and rule not the bodies of the world, neither are they fitted for the government of inferior things, but infuse the light received from God unto the inferior orders, and distribute every one's duty to all of them. The celestial intelligences do next follow these in the second order, which they call worldly angels, *viz.* being appointed, besides the divine worship for the spheres of the world, and for the government of every heaven and star; whence they are divided into so many orders as there are heavens in the world, and as there are stars in the heavens. And they called these *Saturnine*, who rule the heaven of *Saturn*, and *Saturn* himself; others *Jovial*, who rule the heaven of *Jupiter*, and *Jupiter* himself; and in like manner they name different angels, as well for the name as the virtue of the other stars; and because the old astrologers maintained fifty-five motions, therefore they invented so many intelligences or angels. They placed also in the starry heaven angels who

might

A Deceiver

Apollyon

Vessells of Iniquity

Belial

Designed by F. Barrett.

Engraved by R. Griffith

Heads of Evil
Damons.
Nº 2.

Vessels of Wrath

Theutus

Asmodeus

The Incubus

Designed by F. Barrett.

Engraved by R. Griffith.

might rule the signs, triplicities, decans, quinaries, degrees and stars ; for although the school of Peripatetics assign one only intelligence to each of the orbs of the stars, yet seeing every star and small part of the heaven hath its proper and different power and influence, it is necessary also that it have its ruling intelligence which may confer power and operate ; therefore they have established twelve princes of the angels, who rule the twelve signs of the zodiac, and thirty-six who may rule so many decans, and seventy-two who may rule so many quinaries of heaven, and the tongues of men and nations, and four who may rule the triplicities and elements, and seven governors of the whole world, according to the seven planets ; and they have given to all of them *names* and *seals*, which they call *characters*, and used them in their invocations, incantations and carvings, describing them in the instruments of their operations, *images, plates, glasses, rings, papers, wax-lights*, and such like. And if at any time they operated for the sun, they invocated by the name of the sun and by the names of solar angels, and so of the rest. Thirdly, they established angels as ministers for the disposing of those things which are below, which Origen called certain invisible powers, to which those things which are on earth are committed to be disposed of. For sometimes, they being visible to none do direct our journies and all our business, are often present at battles, and, by secret helps, do give the desired success to their friends ; for, at their pleasure, they can procure prosperity, and inflict adversity. In like manner they distribute these into more orders, so as some are fiery, some watery, some aërial, some terrestrial ; which four species of angels are computed according to the four powers of the celestial souls, *viz.* the mind, reason, imagination, and vivifying and moving nature ; hence the fiery follow the mind of the celestial souls, whence they concur to the contemplation of more sublime things ; but the aërial follow reason, and favour the rational faculty, and, after a certain manner, separate it from the sensitive and vegetative ; therefore it serves for an active life, as the fiery the contemplative ; but the watery follow the imagination, serve for a voluptuous life ; the earthly following nature, favours vegetable nature. Moreover, they distinguish also this kind of angels into *saturnine* and *jovial*, according to the names of the stars and the heavens ;

vens; farther, some are oriental, some occidental, some meridional, some
septentrional. Moreover, there is no part of the world destitute of the proper assistance of these angels, not because they are alone, but because they
reign there especially; for they are every where, although some especially operate, and have their influence in this place, some elsewhere;
neither truly are these things to be understood as though they were subject to the influence of the stars, but as they have correspondence with
the heaven above the world, from whence especially all things are directed,
and to which all things ought to be conformable; whence, as these angels
are appointed for diverse stars, so also for diverse places and times; not that
they are limited to any place or time, neither by the bodies which they are
appointed to govern, but because the Divine Wisdom hath so decreed; therefore they favour more, and patronize those bodies, places, times, stars: so
they have called some diurnal, some nocturnal, others meridional. In like
manner some are called woodmen, some mountaineers, some fieldmen, some
domestics: hence the gods of the woods, country gods, satyrs, familiars,
fairies of the fountains, fairies of the woods, nymphs of the sea, the Naïades,
Nereïdes, Dryades, Piërides, Hamadryades, Patumides, Hinnides Agapte,
Pales, Parcades, Dodonæ, Fanilæ, Levernæ, Parcæ, Muses, Aonides, Casta-
lides, Heliconides, Pegasides, Meonides, Phebiades, Camenæ, the graces,
the genii, hobgobblins, and such like; whence the vulgar call them supe-
riors, some the demi-gods and goddesses: some of these are so familiar and
acquainted with men, that they are even affected with human perturbations;
by whose instructions Plato thinks that men do oftentimes wonderful things,
even as by the instruction of men; some beasts which are most nigh to us,
apes, dogs, elephants, do often strange things above their species; and they
who have written the chronicles of the Danes and Norwegians, do testify
that spirits of several kinds in those regions are subject to men's commands;
moreover, some of these appear corporeal and mortal, whose bodies are begotten and die; yet to be long-lived is the opinion of the Egyptians and Platonists, and especially approved by Proclus, Plutarch also, and Demetrius the
philosopher, and Æmilianus the rhetorician, affirm the same; therefore of
these

these spirits of the third kind, as the opinion of the Platonists is, they report that there are so many legions as there are stars in the heaven, and so many spirits in every legion as in heaven itself stars : but there are, (as Athanasius delivers,) who think, that the true number of the good spirits is according to the number of men, ninety-nine parts, according to the parable of the hundred sheep; others think only nine parts, according to the parable of the ten goats; others suppose the number of the angels equal with men, because it is written, he that hath appointed the bounds of the people according to the number of the angels of God; and concerning their number many have written many things; but the latter theologians, following the masters of the sentences, *Austin* and *Gregory*, easily resolve themselves, saying, that the number of the good angels transcendeth human capacity; to the which, on the contrary, innumerable unclean spirits do correspond, there being so many in the inferior world as pure spirits in the superior; and some divines affirm that they have received this by revelation. Under these they place a kind of spirits subterraneous or obscure, which the Platonists call angels that failed, revengers of wickedness and ungodliness, according to the decree of the divine justice; and they call them evil angels and wicked spirits, because they often annoy and hurt, even of their own accord. Of these also they reckon more legions; and, in like manner, distinguishing them according to the names of the stars and elements, and parts of the world, they place over them kings, princes, and rulers; and the names of them : of these, four most mischievous kings rule over the other, according to the four parts of the world. Under these many more princes of legions govern, and many private officers; hence the *Gorgones, Statenocte,* the Furies; hence *Tisiphone, Alecto, Megæra, Cerberus.* They of this kind of spirits, *Porphyry* says, inhabit a place nigh the earth, yea within the earth itself; there is no mischief which they dare not commit; they have altogether a violent and hurtful nature, therefore they plot, and endeavour violent and sudden mischiefs; and when they make incursions, sometimes they lie hid, and sometimes offer open violence, and are very much delighted in all such things done wickedly and mischievously.

CHAP.

CHAP. VII.

THERE are some of the school of theologians, who distribute the evil spirits into nine degrees, as contrary to the nine orders of angels. Therefore, the first of these, which are called false gods, who, usurping the name of God, would be worshipped for gods, and require sacrifices and adorations; as that devil who said to Christ, " If thou wilt fall down and worship me, I will give thee all these things," shewing him all the kingdoms of the world; and the prince of these is he who said, I will ascend above the height of the clouds, and will be like to the Most High, who is called Beelzebub, that is, an old god. In the second place, follow the spirits of lies, of which sort was he who went forth, and was a lying spirit in the mouth of the prophet of Ahab; and the prince of these is the serpent Pytho, from whence Apollo is called Pythius, and that woman a Pythoness, or witch, in Samuel, and the other in the gospel, who had Pytho in her belly. Therefore, these kind of devils join themselves to the oracles, and delude men by divinations and predictions, so that they may be deceived. In the third order, are the vessels of iniquity, which are called vessels of wrath : these are the inventors of evil things, and all wicked arts ; as in Plato, that devil Theutus, who taught cards and dice ; for all wickedness, malice, and deformity, proceeds from these, of which in *Genesis*, in the benedictions of Simeon and Levi, Jacob said, " vessels of iniquity are in their habitations, into their counsel let not my soul come ; " which the *Psalmist* calls vessels of death, *Isaiah*, vessels of fury ; and *Jeremiah*, vessels of wrath ; *Ezekiel*, vessels of destroying and slaying ; and their prince is Belial, which signifies, without a yoke, and disobedient, a prevaricator, and an apostate ; of whom Paul to the Corinthians says, " what agreement has Christ with Belial ? " Fourthly, follow the revengers of evil, and their prince is Asmodeus, *viz.* causing judgment. After these, in the fifth place, come the deluders, who imitate miracles, and serve

conjurers

Ophis.

The Spirit Antichrist.

F. Barrett Del.   Pub. by Lackington & Allen.   R. Griffith Sculp.

Astaroth

Abaddon

Mammon

F. Barrett Del.   Pub. by Lackington & Allen.   P. Griffith Scu.

conjurers and witches, and seduce the people by their miracles, as the serpent
seduced Eve, and their prince is Satan, of whom it is written in the Revelation,
" that he seduces the whole world, doing great signs, and causing fire to descend
from heaven in the sight of men ; seducing the inhabitants of the earth by
these signs, which are given him to do."   Sixthly, the aerial powers offer
themselves and join themselves to thunder and lightning, corrupting the air,
causing pestilences, and other evils ; in the number of which are the four
angels of whom the Revelations speak, to whom it is given to hurt the
earth and the sea, holding the four winds from the four corners of the earth ;
and their prince is called Meririm : he is the meridian devil, a boiling spirit,
a devil raging in the south, whom *Paul,* to the *Ephesians,* calls " the prince of
the power of the air, and the spirit which works in the children of disobe-
dience."   The seventh mansion the furies possess, who are powers of evil,
discords, war, and devastation ; whose name in the Revelation is called in
Greek, *Apollyon ;* in the Hebrew, *Abaddon,* that is, destroying and wasting.
In the eighth place are the accusers or inquisitors, whose prince is Astaroth,
that is, a searcher out ; in the Greek language he is called Diabolus, that is,
an accuser or calumniator ; which in the Revelation is called the " accuser of
the brethren, accusing them night and day before the face of God."   Moreover, the tempters and ensnarers have the last place ; one of which is
present with every man, which we call the evil genius, and their prince is
Mammon, which is interpreted covetousness.   But we of the Cabala unani-
mously maintain that evil spirits do wander up and down this inferior world,
enraged against, all whom we call devils ; of whom *Austin,* in his first
book of the Incarnation of the Word, to *Januarius,* says, concerning the devils
and his angels contrary to virtues, the ecclesiastical preachers have taught that
there are such things, but what they are, and who they are, he has not clear
enough expounded : yet there is this opinion among them, that this devil
was an angel, and being made an apostate, persuaded many of the angels to
fall with him, who to this day are called his angels.   Greece, notwithstanding,
thinks not that these are damned, nor that they are all purposely evil ; but
that from the creation of the world the dispensation of things is ordained by
this

this means, that the tormentiing of sinful souls is made over to them. The other theologians say, that no devil was created evil, but that they were driven and cast out of heaven from the orders of good angels, for their pride; whose fall not only our and the *Hebrew theologians*, but also the *Assyrians*, *Arabians*, *Egyptians*, and *Greeks*, do confirm by their tenets. *Pherycies*, the *Assyrian*, describes the fall of the devils; and *Ophis*, that is, the devilish serpent, was the head of that rebelling army; Trismegistus sings the same fall, in his Pimander; and Homer, under the name of Ararus, in his verses; and Plutarch, in his Discourse on Usury, signifies that Empedocles knew that the fall of the devils was in this manner; the devils themselves often confess their fall. They being cast out into this valley of misery, some that are near to us wander up and down in this obscure air; others inhabit lakes, rivers, and seas; others the earth, and terrify earthly things, and invade those who dig wells and metals, cause the gaping of the earth, to strike together the foundations of the mountains, and vex not only men but also other creatures; some being content with laughter and delusion only, do contrive rather to weary men than to hurt them; some heightening themselves to the length of a giant's body, and again shrinking themselves down to the smallest of pigmies, and changing themselves into different forms, to disturb men with vain fear; others study lies and blasphemies, as we read of one in third book of Kings, saying, "I will go forth and be a lying spirit in the mouth of all the prophets of Ahab." But the worst sort of devils are those who lie in wait, and overthrow passengers in their journies, and rejoice in wars and effusion of blood, and afflict men with most cruel stripes: we read of such in *Matthew*, "for fear of whom no man dare pass that way." Moreover, the Scripture reckons up *nocturnal*, *diurnal*, and *meridional* devils; and describes other spirits of wickedness by different names, as we read in *Isaiah* of satyrs, screech-owls, sirens, storks, owls; and in the *Psalms*, of asps, basilisks, lions, dragons; and in the *Gospel*, we read of scorpions, and Mammon, and the prince of this world, and rulers of darkness, of all whom Beelzebub is the prince, whom the Scripture calls the prince of wickedness.

CHAP.

C H A P. VIII.

OF THE ANNOYANCE OF EVIL SPIRITS, AND THE PRESERVATION WE HAVE FROM GOOD SPIRITS.

IT is the opinion of divines, that all evil spirits are of that nature, that they hate God as well as man ; therefore Divine Providence has set over us more pure spirits, with whom he hath entrusted us, as with shepherds and governors, that they should daily help us, and drive away evil spirits from us, and curb and restrain them, that they should not hurt us, as they would otherwise ; as is read in *Tobias*, that *Raphael* did apprehend the demon called *Asmodeus*, and bound him in the wilderness of the Upper Egypt. Of these, Hesiod says, there are 30,000 of Jupiter's immortal spirits living on the earth, who are the keepers of mortal men, who, that they might observe justice and merciful deeds, having clothed themselves with air, go to and fro every where on the earth. For there is no potentate could be safe, nor any woman continue uncorrupted, no man in this vale of ignorance could come to the end appointed to him by God, if good spirits did not secure us, or if evil spirits should be permitted to satisfy the wills of men ; as therefore among the good there is a proper keeper or protector deputed to every one, corroborating the spirit of the man to good; so of evil spirits, there is sent forth an enemy ruling over the flesh and desire thereof; and the good spirit fights for us as a preserver against the enemy and flesh. Now man, between these contenders is in the middle, and left in the hand of his own counsel, to whom he will give victory : we cannot therefore accuse angels, or deny free-will, if they do not bring the nations entrusted to them to the knowledge of the true God and true piety, but suffer them to fall into errors and perverse worship ; it is to be imputed to themselves, who have, of their own accord, declined from the right path, adhering to the spirits of error, giving victory to the devil : for it is in the hand of man to adhere to whom he

Book II.　　　　　　　　　　　　　　　　　　pleases,

pleases, and overcome whom he will ; by whom if once the devil be overcome, he is made his servant, and being overcome, cannot fight any more
with another, as a wasp that has lost his sting. To which opinion Origen
assents, in his book Periarchon, concluding that the saints fight against evil
spirits, and overcoming, do lessen their army ; neither can he that is overcome by any molest any more. As therefore there is given to every man a
good spirit, so there is given to every man an evil diabolical spirit, whereof each
seeks an union with our spirit, and endeavours to attract it to itself, and to be
mixed with it, as wine with water ; the good indeed, through all good
works comfortable to itself, change us into angels by uniting us ; as it is
written of John the Baptist in Malachi, " behold I send my angel before
thy face ; " of which transmutation and union it is written elsewhere, he that
adheres to God is made one spirit with him. An evil spirit also, by evil
works, studies to make us conformable to itself, and unite us, as *Christ* says
of *Judas*, " Have not I chosen twelve, and one of you is a devil ? " And
this is that which *Hermes* says, when a spirit hath influence on the soul of man,
he scatters the seed of his own notion, whence such a soul, being sown with
seeds, and full of fury, brings forth thence wonderful things, and whatsoever
are the offices of spirits : for when a good spirit hath influence on a holy
soul, it does exalt it to the light of wisdom ; but an evil spirit being trans-
fused into a wicked soul, doth stir it up to theft, to man-slaughter, to lust,
and whatsoever are the offices of evil spirits. Good spirits, as Jamblicus
says, purge the souls most perfectly, and some bestow upon us other good
things : they being present, do give health to the body, virtue to the soul, and
security ; what is mortal in us they take away, cherish heat, and make it
more efficacious to life ; and, by an harmony, do always infuse light into an
intelligible mind. But whether there be many keepers of a man, or one
alone, theologians differ among themselves : *we* think there are more, the
prophet saying, " he hath given his angels a charge concerning thee, that
they should keep thee in all thy ways," which, as Hierome says, is to be
understood of any man, as well as of Christ. All men, therefore, are
governed by the ministry of different angels, and are brought to any degree
of

of virtue, deserts, and dignity, who behave themselves worthy of them ; but they who carry themselves unworthy of them, are deposed and thrust down, as well by evil spirits as good spirits, unto the lowest degree of misery, as their evil merits shall require ; but they that are attributed to the sublimer angels are preferred before other men ; for angels having the care of them, exalt them, and subject others to them by a certain occult power, which, although neither of them perceive, yet he that is subjected feels a certain yoke of presidency, of which he cannot easily quit himself ; yea, he fears and reverences that power, which the superior angels make to flow upon inferiors, and with a certain terror bring the inferiors into a fear of presidency. This did Homer seem to be sensible of, when he says, that the Muses begot of Jupiter, did always, as inseparable companions, assist the kings begot of Jupiter, speaking figuratively, who by them were made venerable and magnificent : so we read that M. Antoninus being formerly joined in singular friendship with Octavius Augustus, were accustomed always to play together ; but when, as always, Augustus always went away conqueror, a certain magician counselled M. Antoninus thus : " O Anthony, what dost thou do with that young man ? Shun and avoid him, for although thou art older than he, and art more skilful than he, and art better descended than he, and hath endured the wars of more emperors, yet thy *Genius* doth much dread the *Genius* of this young man, and thy fortune flatters his fortune ; unless thou shalt shun him, it seems wholly to decline to him." Is not the prince like other men ? how should other men fear and reverence him, unless a divine terror should exalt him, and striking a fear into others, depress them, that they should reverence him as a prince ? Wherefore we must endeavour, that, being purified by doing well, and following sublime things, and choosing opportune times and seasons, we be entrusted or committed to a degree of sublimer and more potent angels, who taking care of us, we may deservedly be preferred before others.

CHAP.

CHAP. IX.

THAT THERE IS A THREEFOLD KEEPER OF MAN, AND FROM WHENCE EACH OF THEM PROCEED.

EVERY man hath a threefold good demon as a proper keeper or preserver, the one whereof is holy, another of the nativity, and the other of profession. The holy demon is one, according to the doctrine of the *Egyptians*,
assigned to the rational soul, not from the stars or planets, but from a
supernatural cause—from God himself, the president of demons, being
universal and above nature. This directs the life of the soul, and does always
put good thoughts into the mind, being always active in illuminating us,
although we do not always take notice of it ; but when we are purified and
live peaceably, then it is perceived by us, then it does, as it were, speak
with us, and communicates its voice to us, being before silent, and studies
daily to bring us to a sacred perfection. So it falls out that some profit more
in any science, or art, or office, in a less time and with little pains, when
another takes much pains and studies hard, and all in vain ; and although no
science, art or virtue, is to be contemned, yet that you may live prosperously,
carry on thy affairs happily, in the first place, know thy good *genius*, and his
nature, and what good the celestial disposition promises thee, and God the distributer of all these, who distributes to each as he pleases, and follow the beginnings of these, profess these, be conversant in that virtue to which the most
high distributer doth elevate and lead thee ; who made *Abraham* excel in justice and clemency, *Isaac* with fear, *Jacob* with strength, *Moses* with meekness
and miracles, *Joshua* in war, *Phineas* in zeal, *David* in religion and victory,
Solomon in knowledge and fame, *Peter* in faith, *John* in charity, *Jacob* in devo-
tion, *Thomas* in prudence, *Magdalen* in contemplation, *Martha* in officious-
ness. Therefore in what virtue you think you can most easily be a proficient
in, use diligence to attain to the height thereof, that you may excel in one,
                                                                    when

when in many you cannot, but in the rest endeavour to be as great a proficient as you can; but if thou shalt have the overseers of nature and religion agreeable, thou shalt find a double progress of thy nature and profession; but if they shall be disagreeing, follow the better, for thou shalt better perceive at some time a preserver of an excellent profession than of nativity.

CHAP. X.

OF THE TONGUE OF ANGELS, AND OF THEIR SPEAKING AMONGST THEMSELVES AND WITH US.

WE might doubt whether angels or demons, since they are pure spirits, use any vocal speech or tongue among themselves or to us; but that Paul, in some place says, "if I speak with the tongue of men or angels;"—but what their speech or tongue is, is much doubted by many. For many think that if they use any idiom, it is Hebrew, because that was first of all, and came from heaven, and was before the confusion of languages in Babylon, in which the law was given by God the Father, and the gospel was preached by Christ the Son, and so many oracles were given to the prophets by the Holy Ghost; and seeing all tongues have and do undergo various mutations and corruptions, this alone does always continue inviolated. Moreover, an evident sign of this opinion is, that though this demon and intelligence do use the speech of those nations with whom they do inhabit, yet, to them who understand it, they never speak in any idiom but in this alone, viz. Hebrew. But now, how angels speak, it is hid from us, as they themselves are. Now, to us, that we may speak, a tongue is necessary with other instruments; as the jaws, palate, lips, teeth, throat, lungs, the *aspera arteria*, and muscles of the breast, which have the beginning of motion from the soul. But if I speak at a distance to another, he

must

must use a louder voice ; but, if near, he whispers in my ear, as if he should be coupled to the hearer, without any noise, as an image in the eye or glass. So souls going out of the body, so angels, so demons speak ; and what man does with a sensible voice, they do by impressing the conception of the speech in those to whom they speak after a better manner than if they should express it in an audible voice. So the Platonist says, that Socrates perceived his demon by sense, indeed, but not of this body, but by the sense of the *etherial body* concealed in this ; after which manner *Avicen* believes the angels were wont to be seen and heard by the prophets. That instrument, whatsoever the virtue be, by which one spirit makes known to another spirit what things are in his mind, is called by the *apostle Paul*, the *tongue of angels*. Yet oftentimes they send forth an audible voice, as they that cried at the ascension of the Lord, Ye men of Galilee, why stand ye here gazing unto the heaven ? And in the old law they spake with divers of the fathers with a sensible voice; but this never but when they assumed bodies. But with what senses these spirits and demons hear our invocations and prayers, and see our ceremonies, we are altogether ignorant.

For there is a *spiritual body* of demons every where sensible by nature, so that it touches, sees, hears without any medium, and nothing can be an impediment to it; yet they do not perceive after the same manner as we do, with different organs, but haply as sponges drink in water, so do they all sensible things with their body or some other way unknown to us ; neither are all animals endowed with those organs, for we know that many want ears, yet we know they perceive a sound, but after what manner we know not.

CHAP.

C H A P.   X I.

OF THE NAMES OF SPIRITS, AND THEIR VARIOUS IMPOSITION, AND OF THE SPIRITS THAT
ARE SET OVER THE STARS, SIGNS, CORNERS OF THE HEAVEN, AND THE ELEMENTS.

MANY and different are the names of good and bad spirits ; but their proper
and true names, as those of the stars, are known to God alone, who only numbers the multitude of stars, and calls them by their names, whereof none can
be known by us but by divine revelation ; very few are expressed to us in sacred
writ.   But the masters of the Hebrews think, that the names of angels are
imposed on them by Adam, according to that which is written, " the Lord
brought all things which he had made unto Adam, that he should name them,
and as he called any thing, so the name of it was."   Hence the Hebrew
Mecubals think, together with Magicians and Cabalists, that it is in the power of
man to impose names upon spirits, but of such a man only who is dignified and
elevated to this virtue by some divine gift or sacred authority : but because a
name that may express the nature of divinity, or the whole virtue of angelical
essences, cannot be made by any human voice, therefore names for the most part
are put upon them from their works, signifying some certain office or effect
which is required by the quire of spirits ; which name then, and not otherwise, obtains efficacy and virtue to draw any spiritual substance from above, or
beneath, to make any desired effect.

I have seen and known some writing on virgin parchment the name and
seal of some spirit in the hour of the moon, which afterwards he gave to
be devoured by a water-frog, and had muttered over some verse ; the frog
being let go into the water, rains and showers presently followed.   I saw also
the same man inscribing the name of another spirit with the seal thereof in
the hour of Mars, which was given to a crow, who, being let go, after a verse
muttered over, there followed from that part of the heaven whither it flew,
lightnings, shaking, and horrible thunders, with thick clouds ; neither were
those

those names of spirits of an unknown tongue, neither did they signify any thing else but their offices; of this kind are the names of those angels, *Raziel, Gabriel, Michael, Raphael, Haniel,* which is as much as to say the vision of God, the virtue of God, the strength of God, the medicine of God, the glory of God. In like manner, in the offices of evil demons are read their names, *viz. a player, a deceiver, a dreamer, a fornicator,* and many such like. So we receive from many of the ancient fathers of the Hebrews the names of angels set over the planets and signs; over *Saturn, Zaphiel*; over *Jupiter, Zadkiel*; over *Mars, Camael*; over the *Sun, Raphael*; over *Venus, Haniel*; over *Mercury, Michael*; over the *Moon, Gabriel.* These are those seven spirits which always stand before the face of God, to whom is entrusted the disposing the whole celestial and terrene kingdoms which are under the moon : for these (as the more curious theologians say) govern all things by a certain vicissitude of hours, days, and years; as the astrologers teach concerning the planets which they are set over, which Mercurius Trismegistus calls the seven governors of the world, who, by the heavens as by instruments, distribute the influences of all the stars and signs upon their inferiors. There are some who ascribe them to the stars by names somewhat differing, saying, that over Saturn is set an intelligence called *Oriphael,* over Jupiter *Zachariel,* over Mars *Zamael,* over the Sun *Michael,* over Venus *Anael,* over Mercury *Raphael,* over the Moon *Gabriel.* And every one of these governs the world 354 years and four months; and the government begins from the intelligence of *Saturn*; afterwards, in order, the intelligences of *Venus, Jupiter, Mercury, Mars,* the *Moon,* and the *Sun* reign, and the government returns to the spirit of Saturn.

Tritemius writ to Maximilian Cæsar a special treatise concerning these, which he that will thoroughly examine may from thence draw great knowledge of future times.   *Over the twelve signs are set these, *viz.* over *Aries, Malahidael*; over *Taurus, Asmodel*; over *Gemini, Ambriel*; over *Cancer, Muriel*; over *Leo, Verchiel*; over *Virgo, Hamaliel*; over *Libra, Zuriel*; over *Scorpio, Barchiel*; over *Sagittarius, Advachiel*; over *Capricorn, Hanael*; over *Aquarius, Cambiel*; over *Pisces, Barchiel.* Of these spirits set over the planets and signs,

* TRITEMIUS on Spirits.

signs, *John* made mention of in the Revelation, speaking of the former in the beginning; and the seven spirits which are in the presence of the throne of God, which I find are set over the seven planets, in the end of the book, where he describes the platform of the heavenly city, saying, that on the twelve gates thereof are twelve angels. There are again twenty-eight angels, who rule in the twenty-eight mansions of the moon, whose names are these; *Geniel, Enediel, Anixiel, Azariel, Gabriel, Dirachiel, Scheliel, Amnediel, Barbiel, Ardefiel, Neciel, Abdizuel, Jazeriel, Ergediel, Atliel, Azeruel, Adriel, Egibiel, Amutiel, Kyriel, Bethnael, Geliel, Requiel, Abrinael, Aziel, Tagriel, Atheniel, Amnixiel.* There are also four princes of the angels, which are set over the four winds, and over the four parts of the world. Michael is placed over the east-wind, Raphael over the west, Gabriel over the north, Nariel, who by some is called Ariel, is over the south. There are also assigned to the elements these, *viz.* to the air *Cherub*, to the water *Tharsis*, to the earth *Ariel*, to the fire *Seraph*. Now every one of these spirits is a great prince, and has much power and freedom in the dominion of his own planets and signs, and in their times, years, months, days and hours; and in their elements, and parts of the world, and winds. And every one of them rules over many legions; and after the same manner, among evil spirits, there are four, who, as most potent kings, are set over the rest, according to the four parts of the world, whose names are these, *viz. Urieus,* king of the east; *Amaymon,* king of the south; *Paymon,* king of the west; *Egin,* king of the north; which the Hebrew doctors perhaps call more rightly thus, *Samuel, Azazel, Azael,* and *Mahazuel,* under whom many others rule as princes of legions and rulers. Likewise there are innumerable demons of private offices. Moreover, the ancient *theologians* of the Greeks reckon up six demons, which they call *Telchines,* others *Alastores*; which bearing ill-will to men, take up water out of the river *Styx* with their hands, sprinkle it upon the earth, whence follow calamities, plagues, and famines; and these are said to be *Acteus, Megalezius, Ormenus, Lycus, Nicon, Mimon.* But he that desires to know exactly the distinct names, offices, places, and times of angels, and evil demons, let him inquire into the book of *Rabbi Simon* of the Temples, and in his book of Lights, and in his treatise of the Greatness of Stature,

Book II.　　　　　　　　　　　　　　　　　　and

and in the treatise of the Temples of *Rabbi Ishmael,* and in almost all the commentaries of his book of Formation, and he shall find it written at large concerning them.

C H A P. XII.

THE CABALISTS DRAW FORTH THE SACRED NAMES OF ANGELS FROM SACRED WRIT, AND OF THE SEVENTY-TWO ANGELS, WHO BEAR THE NAMES OF GOD; WITH THE TABLES OF ZIRUPH AND THE COMMUTATIONS OF NAMES AND NUMBERS.

THERE are also other sacred names of good and evil spirits deputed to each office of much greater efficacy than the former, which the Cabalists draw from sacred writ, according to that art which we teach concerning them; as also certain names of God are drawn forth out of certain places : the general rule of these is, that wheresoever any thing of divine essence is expressed in the Scripture, from that place the name of God may be gathered ; but in what place soever in the Scripture the name of God is found expressed, then mark what office lies under that name ; wheresoever therefore the Scripture speaks of the office or work of any spirit, good or bad, from thence the name of that spirit, whether good or bad, may be gathered ; this unalterable rule being observed, that of good spirits we receive the names of good spirits, of evil the names of evil : and let us not confound black with white, nor day with night, nor light with darkness, which, by these verses as by an example, is manifest :

" Let them be as dust before the face of the wind ; and let the angel of the Lord scatter them : let their ways be darkness and slippery and let the angel of the Lord pursue them."

יהיו במוץ ינפל רות ומאלאף יהוהדההה
יהידרכם הכף והלק לקות ומלאף יהוה דרפﬞﬞﬞ

in the xxxvth Psalm with the Hebrews, but with us, the xxxivth ; of which the names of those angels are drawn, מידאל *Midael,* and מיראל *Miriael,*

of

of the order of warriors; so of that verse, "*thou shalt set over him the wicked, and Satan shall stand at his right-hand*," out of Psalm cix. with the Hebrews, but with the Latins, cviii.

חפקר עליו רשע וישטן יאמלאל ימינו

is extracted the name of the evil spirit *Schii*, ישעי, which signifies a spirit that is a worker of engines. There is a certain text in Exodus contained in three verses, whereof every one is written with seventy-two letters, beginning thus; the first *Vajisa*, ויסע, the second *Vajabo*, ויבא, the third *Vajot*, וים; which are extended into one line, *viz.* the first and the third from the left-hand to the right, but the middle in a contrary order, beginning from the right to the left, is terminated on the left-hand; then each of the three letters being subordinate the one to the other, make one name, which are seventy-two names, which the Hebrews called *Schemhamphoræ*, to which if the divine name El אל or Jah יהה be added, they produce seventy-two trisyllable names of angels, whereof every one carries the great name of God, as it is written, "my angel shall go before thee; observe him, for my name is in him." And these are those that are set over the seventy-two celestial quinaries, and so many nations and tongues, and joints of man's body, and cooperate with the seventy-two seniors of the synagogue, and so many disciples of Christ: and their names, according to the extraction which the Cabalists make, are manifest in the following table, according to the manner which we have mentioned.

Now there are many other ways of making *Schemhamphoræ* out of those verses; as when all three are written in a right order, one after the other, from the right to the left, besides those which are extracted by the tables of Ziruph, and the tables of commutations, of which we made mention of before. Because these tables serve for all names, as divine, so angelical, we shall therefore subjoin them to this chapter.

These are the seventy-two angels, bearing the name of God, *Schemhamphoræ*.

For the tables, &c. see the annexed Plates, No. 1, 2, 3, 4.

C H A P.

C H A P. XIII.

THE ancient magicians taught an art of finding out the name of a spirit to any desired effect, drawing it from the disposition of the heavens ; as, for example, any celestial harmony being proposed to thee, to make an image or a ring, or any other work to be done under any constellation, if thou wilt find out the spirit that is the ruler of that work, the figure of the heaven being erected, cast forth letters in their number and order, from the degree of the ascendant, according to the succession of signs through each degree, by filling the whole circle of the heavens ; then those letters which fall into the places of the stars, the aid of which you would use, being according to the number and power of those stars marked without into number and order, make the name of a good spirit. But if thou wilt do so from the beginning of a degree falling *against* the progress of the signs, the resulting spirit shall be evil. By this art some of the Hebrews and Chaldean masters teach that the nature and name of any genius may be found out ; as for example, the degree of the ascendant of any one's nativity being known, and the other corners of the heaven being co-equated, then let that which has the most dignities of planets in those four corners, which the *Arabians* call *Almutez*, be first observed among the rest ; and according to that in the second place, that which shall be next to it in the number of dignities, and so in order the rest of them, which obtain any dignity in the aforesaid corners.

This order being used, you may know the true place and degree of them in the heavens, beginning from the degree of the ascendant through each degree, according to the order of signs, to cast twenty-two of the letters of the Hebrews ; then what letters shall fall into the places of the aforesaid stars, being marked and disposed according to the order found out above in the stars, and

rightly

rightly joined together according to the rules of the Hebrew tongue, make the name of a genius; to which, according to the custom, some *monosyllable* name of Divine Omnipotence, *viz.* El or Jah, is subjoined. But if the casting of the letters be made from an angle of the falling, and against the succession of the signs, and the letters which shall fall in the Nadir (that is the opposite point) of the aforesaid stars be after that order, as are said, joined together, shall make the name of an evil genius.

But the Chaldeans proceed another way, for they take not the Almutez of the angles but the Almutez of the eleventh house, and do all things as has been said. Now they find out an evil genius from the Almutez of the angle of the twelfth house, which they call an evil spirit, casting from the degree of the falling against the progress of the signs.

CHAP. XIV.

OF THE CALCULATING ART OF SUCH NAMES BY THE TRADITION OF CABALISTS.

THERE is yet another art of these kind of names, which they call calculatory; and it is made by the following tables, by entering with some sacred, divine, or angelical name, in the column of letters descending, by taking those letters which thou shalt find in the common angles under their stars and signs, which being reduced into order, the name of a good spirit is made of the nature of that star or sign under which thou didst enter; but if thou shalt enter in the column ascending, by taking the common angles above the stars and signs marked in the lowest line, the name of an evil spirit is made. And these are the names of spirits of any order of heaven ministering, as of good, so of bad, which you may after this manner multiply into nine names of so many orders; inasmuch as you may, by entering with one name, draw forth another of a spirit

of

of a superior order out of the same, as well of a good as a bad one ; yet the beginning of this calculation depends upon the names of God ; for every word hath a virtue in *magic*, inasmuch as it depends on the word of God, and is thence framed. Therefore we must know that every angelical name must proceed from some primary name of God. Therefore angels are said to bear the name of God, according to that which is written, "because my name is in him ; " therefore that the names of good angels may be discerned from the names of bad, there is wont oftentimes to be added some name of Divine Omnipotence, as *El*, or *On*, or *Jah*, or *Jod*, and to be pronounced together with it : and because *Jah* is a name of beneficence, and *Jod* the name of a deity, therefore these two names are put only to the names of angels ; but the name *El*, because it imports power and virtue, is therefore added, not only to good but bad spirits ; for neither can evil spirits either subsist or do any thing without the virtue of *El*, God. But we must know that common angles of the same star and sign are to be taken, unless entrance be made with a mixt name, as are the names of genii, and those of which it hath been spoken in the preceding chapter, which are made of the dispositions of the heavens, according to the harmony of divers stars. For as often as the table is to be entered with these, the common angle is to be taken under the star or sign of him that enters.

There are moreover some that do so extend those tables that they think also if there be an entrance made with the name of a star, or office, or any desired effect, a demon, whether good or bad, serving to that office or effect may be drawn out ; upon the same account they that enter with the proper name of any person can extract the names of the genii under that star which shall appear to be over such a person as they shall, by his physiognomy, or by the passions and inclinations of his mind, and by his profession and fortune, know him to be either *martial*, or *saturnine*, or *solary*, or of the nature of any other star.

And although such kind of primary names have none or little power by their signification, yet such kind of extracted names, and such as are derived from them, are of very great efficacy ; as the rays of the sun collected in a hollow glass do most intensely burn, the sun itself being scarce warm.

Now

The Cabula.

Shewing at one View the Seventy-two Angels bearing the name of God, Shemhamphora.

Cabiel	Leviah	Hakamiah	Hariel	Mebahel	Ielael	Hahaiah	Lauiah	Aladiah	Haziel	Cahethel	Akhaiah	Lelahel	Mahasiah	Elemiah	Sitael	Ielil	Vehuiah
Monadel	Chavakiah	Lehahiah	Iehuiah	Vasariah	Lecabel	Omael	Reiiel	Seehiah	Ierathel	Haaiah	Nithaiah	Hahuiah	Melahel	Iviael	Nelchael	Pahaliah	Leuviah
Nithael	Nanael	Imamiah	Hahaziah	Daniel	Vehuel	Mihael	Asaliah	Ariel	Saaliah	Ilahiah	Vevaliah	Michael	Hatahel	Ihiazel	Rehael	Haamiah	Aniel
Nevamaih	Haiuil	Ilbamiah	Rochel	Habuiah	Eiael	Menkl	Damabiah	Mochael	Annauel	Iahhel	Umabel	Mixrael	Harahel	Ieilael	Nemamiah	Poiel	Mebahiah

The Cabala

Table 2.° The Right Table of the Commutations.

Cabala
The Averse Table of Commutations.

F. Barrett Del.

R. Griffith Sculp.

Pub. by Lackington & Allen.

Table 4 & 5

The Table of the Combinations of Ziruph.

The Rational Table of Ziruph.

C. Barrett Del.　　　Pub. by Lackington & Allen.　　　R. Griff

Now there is an order of letters in those tables under the stars and signs, almost like that which is with the astrologers, of tens, elevens, twelves. Of this calculatory art *Alphonsus Cyprius* once wrote, and also fitted it to Latin characters; but because the letters of every tongue, as we shewed in the first book, have, in their number, order and figure, a celestial and divine original, I shall easily grant this calculation concerning the names of spirits to be made not only by Hebrew letters, but also *Chaldean, Arabick, Egyptian, Greek* and *Latin*, and many others, the tables being rightly made after the imitation of the presidents.

But here it is objected by many, that it falls out that in these tables men of a differing nature and fortune do oftentimes, by reason of the sameness of name, obtain the same genius of the same name. We must know therefore that it must not be thought absurd, that the same dæmon may be separated from any one soul, and the same be set over more. Besides, as many men have the same name, so also spirits of divers offices or natures may be noted or marked by one name, and by one and the same seal or character, yet in a different respect; for as the serpent does sometimes typify Christ, and sometimes the devil, so the same names and the same seals may be applied sometimes to the order of a good demon, sometimes of a bad one. Lastly, the very ardent intention of the invocator, by which our intellect is joined to the separated intelligences, is the cause that we have sometimes one spirit, sometimes another, (although called upon under the same name,) made obsequious to us.

See the following Plates for the tables of the calculation of the names of spirits, good and bad, under the presidency of the seven planets, and under the order of the twelve militant signs.

CHAP.

CHAP. XV.

OF THE CHARACTERS AND SEALS OF SPIRITS.

WE must now speak of the characters and seals of spirits. Characters are nothing else than certain unknown letters and writings, preserving the secrets of spirits and their names from the use and reading of prophane men, which the ancient called hieroglyphical, or sacred letters, because devoted to the secrets of God only. They accounted it unlawful to write the mysteries of God with those characters which prophane and vulgar things were wrote. Whence Porphyry says, " that the ancients were willing to conceal God and divine virtues, by sensible figures and by those things which are visible, yet signifying invisible things ; " as being willing to deliver great mysteries in sacred letters, and explain them in certain symbolical figures ; as when they dedicated all round things to the world, the sun and the moon, hope and fortune ; a circle to the heavens, and parts of a circle to the moon ; pyramids and obelisks to the fire, a cylinder to the sun and earth.—See the plate.

CHAP. XVI.

ANOTHER WAY OF MAKING CHARACTERS, ACCORDING TO THE CABALISTS.

AMONG the Hebrews I find more fashions of characters, whereof one is most ancient, *viz.* an ancient writing which Moses and the prophets used, the form of which is not rashly to be discovered to any ; for those letters which they use at this day were instituted by Esdras. There is among them a writing which they call celestial, because they shew it placed and figured among the stars.

The Cabala

The Tables for the calculations of the names of Spirits good & bad & under the presidency of the 7 Planets & 12 militant Signs

The entrance of Evil Angels

	☽	☿	♀	☉	♂	♃	♄	The Line of Good
ת	ז	י	ה	ד	ג	ב	א	א
ש	נ	מ	ל	כ	י	ט	ח	ב
ר	ש	ר	ק	צ	פ	ע	ס	ג
ק	ו	ה	ד	ג	ב	א	ת	ד
צ	מ	ל	כ	י	ט	ח	ו	ה
פ	ר	ק	צ	פ	ע	ס	נ	ו
ע	ה	ד	ג	ב	א	ת	ש	ז
ס	ל	כ	י	ט	ח	ז	ו	ח
נ	ק	צ	פ	ע	ס	נ	מ	ט
מ	ד	ג	ב	א	ת	ש	ר	י
ל	כ	י	ט	ח	ז	ו	ה	כ
כ	צ	פ	ע	ס	נ	מ	ל	ל
י	ג	ב	א	ת	ש	ר	ק	מ
ט	י	ט	ח	ז	ו	ה	ד	נ
ח	פ	ע	ס	נ	מ	ל	כ	ס
ז	ב	א	ת	ש	ר	ק	צ	ע
ו	ט	ח	ז	ו	ה	ד	י	פ
ה	פ	ס	נ	מ	ל	כ	י	צ
ד	א	ת	ש	ר	ק	צ	פ	ק
ג	ח	ז	ו	ה	ד	ג	ב	ר
כ	ס	נ	מ	ל	כ	י	ט	ש
א	ת	ש	ר	ק	צ	פ	ע	ת
The Line of Evil	♄	♃	♂	☉	☽	♀	☿	

The entrance of Good Angels

The entrance of the Evil Angels

	♓	♒	♑	♐	♏	♎	♍	♌	♋	♊	♉	♈	The Line of Good
ת	ל	כ	י	ט	ח	ז	ו	ה	ד	ג	ב	א	א
ש	א	ב	ג	ד	ה	ו	ז	ח	ט	י	כ	ל	ב
ר	ב	א	ת	ש	ר	ק	צ	פ	ע	ס	נ	מ	ג
ק	מ	נ	ס	ע	פ	צ	ק	ר	ש	ת	א	ב	ד
צ	נ	מ	ל	כ	י	ט	ח	ז	ו	ה	ד	ג	ה
פ	ג	ד	ה	ו	ז	ח	ט	י	כ	ל	מ	נ	ו
ע	ד	ג	ב	א	ת	ש	ר	ק	צ	פ	ע	ס	ז
ס	ס	ע	פ	צ	ק	ר	ש	ת	א	ב	ג	ד	ח
נ	ע	ס	נ	מ	ל	כ	י	ט	ח	ז	ו	ה	ט
מ	ה	ו	ז	ח	ט	י	כ	ל	מ	נ	ס	ע	י
ל	י	ה	ד	ג	ב	א	ת	ש	ר	ק	צ	פ	כ
כ	פ	צ	ק	ר	ש	ת	א	ב	ג	ד	ה	ו	ל
י	צ	פ	ע	ס	נ	מ	ל	כ	י	ט	ח	ז	מ
ט	ז	ח	ט	י	כ	ל	מ	נ	ס	ע	פ	צ	נ
ח	ח	ז	ו	ה	ד	ג	ב	א	ת	ש	ר	ק	ס
ז	ק	ר	ש	ת	א	ב	ג	ד	ה	ו	ז	ח	ע
ו	ר	ק	צ	פ	ע	ס	נ	מ	ל	כ	י	ט	פ
ה	ט	י	כ	ל	מ	נ	ס	ע	פ	צ	ק	ר	צ
ד	י	ט	ח	ז	ו	ה	ד	ג	ב	א	ת	ש	ק
ג	ש	ת	א	ב	ג	ד	ה	ו	ז	ח	ט	י	ר
ב	ת	ש	ר	ק	צ	פ	ע	ס	נ	מ	ל	כ	ש
א	כ	ל	מ	נ	ס	ע	פ	צ	ק	ר	ש	ת	ת
The Line of Evil	ל	כ	י	ט	ח	ז	ו	ה	ד	ג	ב	א	

The entrance of the Good Angels

The Misterious Characters of Letters deliver'd by Honorious call'd the Theban Alphabet.

A B C D E F G H I K L M

N O P Q R S T V X Y Z

The Characters of Celestial Writing

Lamed Caph Jod Theth Cheth Zain Vau He Daleth Gimel Beth Aleph

Tau Shin Res Kuff Zade Pe Ain Samech Nun Mem

The Writing call'd Malachim.

Caph Jod Theth Cheth Zain Vau He Daleth Gimel Beth Aleph

Pesh Kuff Zade Pe Ain Samech Samech Schin Tau Nun Mem Lamed

The Writing call'd Passing the River.

Lamed Caph Jod Theth Cheth Zain Vau He Daleth Gimel Beth Aleph

Tan Schin Resh Kuff Zade Pe Ain Samech Nun Mem

Powell Del.   Pub. by Lackington & Allen.   R Griffith Sculp.

stars. There is also a writing which they call *Malachim*, or *Melachim*, *i. e.* of angels, or regal; there is also another, which they call the passing through the river, and the characters and figures of all which you may see in the following Plates.

There is another manner among the Cabalists, formerly held in great esteem, but now it is so common that it is placed among prophane things, *viz.* the twenty-seven characters of the Hebrews may be divided into three classes, whereof every one contains nine letters. The first, *viz.* אבגדהוזחט which are the seals or marks of simple numbers and of intellectual things distributed into nine orders of angels. The second hath יכלמנסעפצ, the marks of tens and celestial things in the nine orbs of the heavens. The third hath the other four letters, with the five final, *viz.* קרשתךםןףץ, which are marks of hundreds, and inferior things, *viz.* four simple elements, and five kinds of perfect compounds. They do now and then distribute these three classes into nine chambers, the first is of units, *viz.* intellectual, celestial and elemental. The second is of two's, the third of three's, and so of the rest; these chambers are framed by the intersection of four parallel lines intersecting themselves into right angles, as is expressed in the following Plate, fig. A.

Out of which, being dissected into parts, proceed nine particular figures (See Plate, fig. B.) which are of the nine chambers, characterizing their letters by that Notariacon, which, if it be of one point, shews the first letter of that chamber; if of two, the second; if of three, the third letter; as if you would frame the character, Michael, מיכאל, that comes forth extended with five figures (for which see the Plate C.) which are contracted to three figures, which then are contracted into one, yet the points Notariacon are usually omitted, and then there comes forth such a character of Michael. See fig. D.

There is yet another fashion of characters common to almost all letters and tongues, and very easy, which is by gathering together of letters; as if the name of the angel Michael be given, the characters thereof shall be framed according to the fig. E.

BOOK II.   And

And this fashion among the Arabians is most received ; neither is there any writing which is so readily and elegantly joined to itself as the Arabick. You must know that angelical spirits, seeing they are of a pure intellect, and altogether incorporeal, are not marked with any marks or characters, or any other human signs ; but we, not otherwise knowing their essence or quality, do, from their *names*, or *works*, or otherwise, devote and consecrate to them figures and marks, by which we cannot any way compel them to us, but by which we rise up to them, as not to be known by such characters and figures, and, first of all, we do set our senses, both inward and outward, upon them ; then, by a certain admiration of our reason, we are induced to a religious veneration of them ; and then are wrapt with our whole mind into an ecstatical adoration ; and then with a wonderful belief, an undoubted hope, and quickening love, calling upon them in spirit and truth by true names and characters, do obtain from them that virtue or power which we desire.

C H A P. XVII.

THERE IS ANOTHER KIND OF CHARACTERS, OR MARKS OF SPIRITS, WHICH ARE RECEIVED
ONLY BY REVELATION.

THERE is another kind of character received by revelation only, which can be found out no other way ; the virtue of which characters is from the Deity revealing ; of whom there are some secret works breathing out a harmony of some divinity, or they are, as it were, some certain agreements or compacts of a league between us and them. Of this kind there was a sign shewed to *Constantine*, which was this, *in hoc vince* ; there was another revealed to *Antiochus* in the figure of a Pentangle, which signifies health ; for,
being

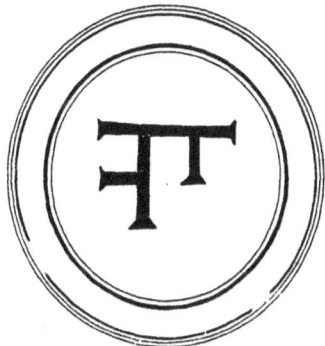

The Cabala

Fig. A

Fig. B

Fig. C

Fig. D

Fig. F

Fig. F. The Cabalistic Character of the Spirit Michael as Composed out of the above Tables A. B. C. D.

being resolved into letters, it speaks the word ὑγίεια, *i. e.* health : in the faith and virtue of which signs, both kings obtained a great victory against their enemies. So Judas, who by reason of that, was afterwards surnamed Machabeus, being to fight with the Jews against *Antiochus Eupator*, received from an angel a notable sign, מכבי, in the virtue of which they first slew 11,000, with an infinite number of elephants, then again 35,000 of their enemies : for that sign did represent the name of *Jehovah*, and was a memorable emblem of the name of seventy-two letters by the equality of number ; and the exposition thereof is מי כמיר באלי מיהית, *i. e.* who is there among thee strong as *Jehovah ?* See Plate, fig. F.

C H A P. XVIII.

ON THE BONDS OF SPIRITS, AND THEIR ADJURATIONS, AND CASTINGS OUT.

THE bond by which spirits are bound, besought, or cast out, are three ; some of them are taken from the elemental world, as when we adjure a spirit by an inferior and natural thing of affinity with or adverse to them ; inasmuch as we would call up or cast them out, as by fumigations of *flowers, herbs, animals, snow, ice,* or by *hell, fire,* and *such like* ; and these also are often mixt with divine praises, and blessings, and consecrations, as appears in the song of the Three Children, and in the psalm, Praise ye the Lord from the heavens, and in the consecration and blessing of the *paschal taper.* This bond works upon the spirits by an apprehensive virtue, under the account of love or hatred, inasmuch as the spirits are present with, or favour, or abhor any thing that is natural or against nature, as these things themselves love or hate one another. The second bond is taken from the celestial world, *viz.* when we adjure them by their heaven, by the stars, by their motions, rays, light, beauty, clearness, excellency, fortitude, influence and wonders, and such like ; and this bond works

upon

upon ſpirits by way of admonition and example. It hath also some command, especially upon the ministering spirits, and those who are of the lowest orders. The third bond is from the intellectual and divine world, which is perfected by religion; that is to say, when we swear by the sacraments, miracles, divine names, sacred seals, and other mysteries of religion ; wherefore this bond is the highest of all and the strongest, working upon the spirits by command and power; but this is to be observed, that as after the universal Providence there is a particular one, and after the universal soul, particular souls; so, in the first place, we invocate by the superior bonds, and by the names and powers which rule the things, then by the inferior and the things themselves. We must know further, that by these bonds, not only spirits, but also all creatures are bound, as tempests, burnings, floods, plagues, diseases, force of arms, and every animal, by assuming them, either by adjuration or deprecation, or benediction, as in the charming of serpents ; besides the natural and celestial, by rehearsing out of the mysteries and religion, the cure of the serpent in terrestrial paradise, the lifting up of the serpent in the wilderness ; likewise by assuming that verse of the 91st Psalm, *thou shalt walk upon the asp and the basilisk, and shalt tread upon the lion and the dragon.*

C H A P. XIX.

BY WHAT MEANS MAGICIANS AND NECROMANCERS CALL FORTH THE SOULS OF THE DEAD.

BY the things which have been already spoken it is manifest, that souls after death do as yet love their body which they left, as those souls do whose bodies want due burial or have left their bodies by violent death, and as yet wander about their carcasses in a troubled and moist spirit, being, as it were, allured by something that hath an affinity with them, the means being known, by which in times past, they were joined to their bodies, they may be easily called forth

and

and allured by the like vapours, liquors and savours, certain artificial lights being also used, songs, sounds, and such like, which moves the imaginative and spiritual harmony of the soul; and sacred invocations, and such like, as belong to religion, ought not to be neglected by reason of the portion of the rational soul which is above nature.

Necromancy has its name because it works on the bodies of the dead, and gives answers by the ghosts and apparitions of the dead, and subterraneous spirits, alluring them into the carcasses of the dead by certain hellish charms, and infernal invocations, and by deadly sacrifices and wicked oblations.

There are two kinds of necromancy : raising the carcasses, which is not done without blood; the other sciomancy, in which the calling up of the shadow only suffices. To conclude, it works all its experiments by the carcasses of the slain and their bones and members, and what is from them ; for there is in these things a spiritual power friendly to them : therefore they easily allure the flowing down of wicked spirits, by reason of the similitude and property of every familiar, by whom the necromancer, strengthened by their help, can do much in human and terrestrial things, and kindle unlawful lusts, cause dreams, diseases, hatred, and such like passions ; to which also they can confer the powers of the soul, which as yet being involved in a moist and turbid spirit, wandering about their cast bodies, can do the same things that the wicked spirits commit, seeing therefore they experimentally find, that the wicked and impure souls violently plucked from their bodies, and of men not expiated, and wanting burial, do stray about carcasses, and are drawn to them by affinity. The witches easily abuse them for effecting witchcraft, alluring these unhappy souls, by the opposition of their body, or by the taking of some parts thereof, and compelling them by their devilish charms, by entreating them by the deformed carcasses dispersed through the wide fields, and the wandering shadows of those who want burials, and by the ghosts sent back from *Acheron*, and the guests of hell, whom untimely death has precipitated into hell, and by the horrible desires of the damned and proud devils, revengers of wickedness. But he who
could

could restore the souls truly to their bodies, must first know what is the proper nature of the soul from whence it went forth, with how many and how great degrees of perfection it is replenished, with what intelligence it is strengthened, by what means diffused into the body, by what harmony it shall be compacted with it, what affinity it hath with God, with the intelligences, with the heavens, elements, and all other things, whose image and resemblance it holds. To conclude, by what influences the body may be knit together again for the raising of the dead, requires all these things which belong not to men, but to God only, and to whom he will communicate them.

C H A P. XX.

OF PROPHETICAL DREAMS.

I CALL that a dream which proceeds either from the spirit of the phantasy and intellect united together, or by the illustration of the agent intellect above our souls, or by the true revelation of some divine power in a quiet and purified mind ; for by this our soul receives true oracles, and abundantly yields prophecies to us; for in dreams we seem both to ask questions, and learn to find them out ; also many doubtful things, many policies, many things unknown, unwished for, and never attempted by our minds, are manifested to us in dreams : also the representation of things unknown, and unknown places appear to us ; and the images of men, both alive and dead, and of things to come, are foretold; and also things which at any time have happened are revealed, which we know not by any report. And these dreams need not any art of interpretation, as those of which we have before spoken, which belong to divination, not to foreknowledge; and it comes to pass that they who see dreams, for the most part, understand them not : for as to see

dreams

dreams is from the strength of *imagination*, so to understand them is from the strength of the understanding. They, therefore, whose intellect being overwhelmed by too much commerce of the flesh is in a dead sleep, or its imaginative or phantastic power or spirit is too dull and unpolished, that it cannot receive the species and representation which flow from the superior intellect; this man, I say, is altogether unfit for the receiving of dreams and prophesying by them.

Therefore it is necessary that he who would receive true dreams should keep a pure undisturbed, and an undisquieted imaginative spirit, and so compose it that it may be made worthy of the knowledge and government by the mind and understanding; for such a spirit is most fit for prophesying, and is a most clear glass of all the images which flow (every where) from all things. When therefore we are sound in body, not disturbed in mind, our intellect not dulled by meats and drinks, not sad through poverty, not provoked through lust, not incited by any vice, not stirred up by wrath or anger, not being irreligiously and prophanely inclined, not given to levity, not lost in drunkenness, but chastely going to bed, fall asleep; then our pure and divine soul, being free from all the evils above recited, and separated from all hurtful thoughts, and now freed by dreaming, is endowed with this divine spirit as an instrument, and doth receive those beams and representations which are darted down, as it were, and shine forth from the Divine Mind into itself; and, as it were in a deifying glass, it does more certain, more clear and efficaciously behold all things than by the vulgar inquiry of the intellect, and by the discourse of reason. The divine powers instructing the soul, being invited to their society by the opportunity of the nocturnal solitariness, neither will that genius be wanting to him when he is awake, which rules all his actions.

Whosoever therefore, by quiet and religious meditation, and by a diet temperate and moderate according to nature, preserves his spirit pure shall very much prepare himself, and by this means become (in a degree) divine and knowing all things, justly merits the same. But whosoever, on the contrary, languishes with a fantastic spirit, he receives not perspicuous and

distant

distant visions; but even as the divine sight, by reason of its vision, being weakened and impaired, judges confusedly and indistinctly, so also when we are overcome with wine and drunkenness, then our spirit, being oppressed with noxious vapours (as a troubled water is apt to appear in various forms) is deceived, and waxes dull; therefore those who would receive oracles by dreams, and those oracles true and certain, I would advise him to abstain one whole day from meat, and three days from wine or any strong liquors, and drink nothing but pure water; for, to sober and religious minds, the pure spirits are adherent, but fly those who are drowned in drunkenness and surfeiting. Although impure spirits do very often administer notable secrets to those who are apparently besotted with wine or liquors; yet all such communications are to be contemned and avoided.

But there are four kinds of true dreams, *viz.* the first, *matutine, i. e.* between sleeping and waking; the second that which one sees concerning another; the third, that whose interpretation is shewn to the same dreamer in the nocturnal vision; and, lastly, the fourth, that which is repeated to the same dreamer in the nocturnal vision.

END OF PART FIRST.

THE

THE PERFECTION AND KEY

OF

THE CABALA,

OR

CEREMONIAL MAGIC.

———

BOOK II. PART II.

———

IN this last book, which we have made the Perfection and Key of all that
has been written, we have given thee the whole and entire practice of
Ceremonial Magic, shewing what is to be done every hour of the day;
so that as by reading what we have heretofore written, thou shalt contem-
plate in theory, here thou shalt be made perfect by experiment and practice:
for in this Key you may behold, as in a mirror, the distinct functions of the
spirits, and how they are to be drawn into communication in all places, seasons, and times.

This then is to be known, that the names of the intelligent presidents
of every one of the planets are constituted after this manner; that it to say,
by collecting together the letters out of the figures of the world from the
rising of the body of the planet, according to the succession of the signs
through the several degrees, and out of the several degrees, from the aspects
of the planet himself, the calculation being made from the degree of
the ascendant.

In like manner are constituted the names of the princes of the evil spirits; they are taken under all the planets of the presidents in a retrograde order, the projection being made contrary to the succession of the signs, from the beginning of the seventh house. Now the name of the supreme and highest intelligence, which many suppose to be the soul of the world, is collected out of the four cardinal points of the figure of the world, after the manner already delivered; and by the opposite and contrary way is known the name of the great demon or evil spirit, upon the four cadent angles.

In like manner you shall understand the names of the great presidential spirits ruling in the air, from the four angles of the succedent houses, so as to obtain the names of the good spirits: the calculation is to be made according to the succession of the signs, beginning from the degree of the ascendant, and to attain the names of the evil spirits by working the contrary way.

You must also observe, that the names of the evil spirits are extracted as well from the names of the good spirits as of the evil: so, notwithstanding, that if we enter the table with the name of a good spirit of the second order, the name of the evil shall be extracted from the order of *princes* and *governors;* but if we enter the table with the name of a good spirit of the third order, or with the name of an evil spirit, a governor, after what manner soever they are extracted, whether by this table or from a celestial figure, the names which do proceed from hence shall be the names of the evil spirits, the ministers of the inferior order.

It is further to be noted, that as often as we enter this table with the good spirits of the second order, the names extracted are of the second order; and if under them we extract the name of an evil spirit, he is of the superior order of the governors. The same order is, if we enter with the name of an evil spirit of the superior. If therefore we enter this table with the names of the spirits of the third order, or with the names of the ministering spirits, as well of the good spirits as of the evil, the names extracted shall be the names of the ministering spirits of the inferior order.

But

But many magicians, men of no small authority, will have the tables of this kind to be extended with *Latin* letters; so that by the same tables also, out of the name of any office or effect, might be found out the name of any spirit, as well good as evil, by the same manner which is above delivered, by taking the name of the office or of the effect in the column of letters, in their own line, under their own star.   And of this practice *Trismegistus* is a great author, who delivered this kind of calculation in Egyptian letters: not improperly also may they be referred to the letters of other tongues, for the reason assigned to the signs; for truly he only is extant of all men who have treated concerning the attaining to the names of spirits.

Therefore the *force, secrecy,* and *power,* in what manner the sacred names of spirits are truely and rightly found out, consisteth in the disposing of vowels, which make the name of a spirit, and wherewith is constituted the true name and right word.   Now this art is thus perfected and brought to pass.   First, we are to take heed to placing the vowels of the letters, which are found by the calculation of the celestial figure, to find the names of the spirits of the second order, presidents and governors: and this, in the good spirits, is thus brought to effect, by considering the stars which do constitute and make the letters, and by placing them according to their order.   First, let the degree of the eleventh house be subtracted from the degree of that star which is first in order, and that which remains thereof, let it be projected from the degree of the ascendant; and where the number ends, there is part of the vowel of the first letter.

Begin therefore to calculate the vowels of these letters according to their number and order, and the vowel which falls in the place of the star, which is the first in order, the same vowel is attributed to the first letter; then afterwards thou shalt find the part of the second letter, by subtracting the degree of a star, which is the second in order from the first star; and that which remains cast from the ascendant.   And this is the part from which you shall begin the calculation of vowels; and that vowel which falls upon the second star the same is the vowel of the second letter: and so consequently thou mayest search out the vowels of the following letters

by

by always subtracting the degree of the following star from the degree of the star next preceding and going before. And, likewise, all calculations and numerations in the names of the good spirits ought to be made according to the succession of the signs. And whereas in calculating the names of the evil spirits, the names of the good spirits are taken from the degree of the eleventh house; in these ought to be taken the degree of the twelfth house. And all numerations and calculations may be made with the succession of the signs, by taking the beginning from the degree of the tenth house.

But in all extractions by tables, the vowels are placed after another manner. In the first place, is taken the certain number of letters, making the name itself, and is thus numbered from the beginning of the column of the first letter, or whereupon the name is extracted; and the letter on which this number falleth is referred to the first letter of the name extracted, by taking the distance of the one from the other, according to the order of the alphabet. But the number of that distance is projected from the beginning of that column, and where it ends there is part of the first vowel; from thence thou shalt calculate the vowels themselves, in their own number and order in the same column; and the vowel which shall fall upon the first letter of a name, the same shall be attributed to that name.

Now thou shalt find the following vowels, by taking the distance from the preceding vowel to the following, and so consequently according to the succession of the alphabet; and the number of that distance is to be numbered from the beginning of his own column, and where he shall cease, there is part of the vowel sought after. From thence therefore must you calculate the vowels, as we have above said, and those vowels which shall fall upon your own letters, are to be attributed to them. If therefore any vowel should happen to fall upon a vowel, the former must give place to the latter: and this you are to understand only of the good spirits. In the evil spirits likewise you may proceed in the same way; except only that you make the numerations after a contrary and backward order, contrary to the succession of the alphabet, and contrary to the order of the columns (that is to say) ascending.

The

The name of good angels, and of every man, which we have before taught how to find out, according to that manner, is of no little authority, nor of a mean foundation. But now we will give thee some other ways illustrated with no vain reasons. One whereof is by taking in the nativity the five places of Hylech; which being noted, the characters of the letters are projected in their order and number, beginning from *Aries*, and those letters which fall upon the degrees of the said places, according to their order and dignity disposed and aspected, make the name of an angel.

There is also another way wherein they take *Almutel*, which is the ruling and governing star over the aforesaid five places, and the projection is to be made from the degree of the ascendant; which is done by gathering together the letters falling upon Almutel, which being placed in order, according to their dignity, make the name of an angel. There is likewise another way used, and very much had in observation from the Egyptians, by making calculations from the degree of the ascendant, and by gathering together the letters according to the Almutel of the eleventh house; which house they call a good demon; which being placed according to their dignities, the names of the angels are constituted.

Now the names of the evil angels are known after the like manner, except only that the projections must be performed contrary to the course and order of the succession of the signs; so that in seeking the names of good spirits, we are to calculate from the beginning of *Aries*; contrariwise, in attaining the names of evil, we ought to account from the beginning of *Libra*. And whereas, in the good spirits, we number from the degree of the ascendant; contrariety, in the evil, we must calculate from the degree of the seventh house.

But according to the Egyptians, the name of this angel is collected according to the Almutel of the twelfth house, which they call an evil spirit. Now all those rites, which are elsewhere already by us delivered in this Book, may be made by the characters of any language. In all which (as we have said before) there is a mystical and divine number, order and figure, from whence it comes to pass, that the same spirit may be called by divers names; but others

are

are discovered from the name of the spirit himself, of the good or evil, by tables formed to this purpose.

Now these celestial characters do consist of lines and heads. The heads are six, according to the six magnitudes of the stars, whereunto the planets likewise are reduced. The first magnitude holds a star with the sun or a cross; the second, with Jupiter, a circular point; the third, with Saturn, a semicircle, a triangle, either crooked, round, or acute; the fourth, with a Mars, a little stroke penetrating the line, either square, straight or oblique; the fifth, with Venus and Mercury, a little stroke or point with a tail ascending or descending; the sixth, with the moon, a point made black, all which you may see in the annexed plate. The heads then being posited according to the site of the stars of the figure of heaven, then the lines are to be drawn out according to the congruency or agreement of their natures. And this you are to understand of the fixed stars. But in the erecting of the planets, the lines are drawn out, the heads being posited according to their course and nature among themselves.—See the Plate, No. 1.

So when a character is to be found, of any celestial image ascending in any degree or face of a sign, which consists of stars of the same magnitude and nature, then the number of these stars being posited according to their place and order, the lines are drawn after the similitude of the image signified, as copiously as the same can be done.

But the characters which are extracted according to the name of a spirit are composed by the table following, by giving to every letter that name which agrees to him out of the table; and although it may appear easy to those that apprehend it, yet there is no small difficulty herein; to wit, when the letter of a name falls upon the line of letters or figures, that we may know which figure or which letter is to be taken. And this may thus be known; if a letter falls upon the line of letters, consider of what number this letter may be in the order of the name, as the second or the third; then how many letters that name contains, as five or seven; and multiply these numbers one after another by themselves, and treble the product; then cast the whole (being
added

N.º 1 Characters of Good Spirits

A Simple point	Round	Starry
Perpendicular	Horizontal	Oblique
Bowed line	Waving line	Toothed
Intersection Right	Inherent	Adherent Separate
Oblig-Intersection Simple	Mixt	Manifold
Perpendicular Right Dexter	Sinister	Newter
A whole Figure	Broken	Half
A Letter inhering	Adhering	Separate

N.º 2 Characters of Evil Spirits

A right line	Crooked	Reflexed
A Simple Figure	Penetrate	Broken
A Right Letter	Retrograde	Inverse'd
Flame	Wind	Water
Amass	Rain	Clay
A Flying thing	A creeping thing	A Serpent
An Eye	A Hand	A Foot
A Crown	A Crest	Horns
A Scepter	A Sword	A Scourge

F. Barrett Del.   Pub. by Lackington & Allen   R Griffith.

added together) from the beginning of the letters according to the succession of the alphabet; and the letter upon which that number shall happen to fall, ought to be placed for a character of that spirit. But if any letter of a name fall upon the line of figures, it is thus wrought: take the number how many this letter is in the order of the name, and let it be multiplied by the number of which this letter is in the order of the alphabet; and, being added together, divide it by nine, and the remainder will shew the figure or number to be placed in the character, and this may be put either in a geometrical or arithmetrical figure of number; which, notwithstanding, ought not to exceed the number of nine, or nine angels.—See the Plate, No. 2.

But the characters which are understood by the revelations of spirits take their virtue from thence, because they are, as it were, certain hidden seals, making the harmony of some divinity: either they are signs of a covenant entered into, and of a promised or plighted faith, or of obedience. And those characters cannot by any other means be found out.

Besides these characters there are certain familiar figures and images of evil spirits, under which forms they are wont to appear, and yield obedience to those who invoke them. And all these characters and images may be seen in the considerations of each day's business, according to the course of the letters constituting the names of spirits themselves; so that if in any letter there is found more than the name of one spirit, his image holds the pre-eminence, the others imparting their own orders; so they which are of the first order, to them is attributed the head, the upper part of the body, according to their own figure; those which are lowest possess the thighs and feet; so likewise the middle letters do attribute like to themselves the middle parts of the body, to give the parts that fit; but if there happen any contrariety, that letter which is the strongest in the number shall bear rule; and if they are equal they all impart equal things. Moreover if any name shall obtain any notable character or instrument out of the table, he shall likewise have the same character in the image.

We may also attain to the knowledge of the dignities of the evil spirits, by the same tables of characters and images: for upon whatsoever spirit falls

any

any excellent sign or instrument out of the table of characters, he possesses that dignity. As if there should be a crown, it shows a kingly dignity; if a crest or plume, a dukedom; if a horn, a county: if without these there be a sceptre, sword, or forked instrument, it shows rule and authority. Likewise out of the table of images you shall find them who bear the chief kingly dignity: from the crown judge dignity; and from the instruments, rule and authority.

Lastly, they which bear a human shape and figure have a greater dignity than those which appear under the forms and images of beasts. They likewise who ride do excel them which appear on foot. And thus, according to all their commixtures, you may judge the dignity and excellency of spirits, one before another. Moreover, you must understand that the spirits of the inferior order, of what dignity soever, they are always subject to the spirits of the superior order; likewise that it is not incongruent for their kings and dukes to be subject and minister to the presidents of the superior order.

Of Magic Pentacles and their Composition.

WE now proceed to speak of the holy and sacred Pentacles and Seals. For these pentacles are certain holy signs and characters, preserving us from evil chances and events, helping and assisting us to bind, exterminate, and drive away evil spirits, alluring the good spirits, and reconciling them to us. These pentacles consist either of characters of good spirits of the superior order, or of sacred pictures of holy letters or revelations, with apt and proper versicles, which are composed either of geometrical figures and holy names of God, according to the course and manner of many of them, or they are compounded of all of them, or many of them mixed. The characters which are useful for us to constitute and make the pentacles are the characters of

the

the good spirits, chiefly of the good spirits of the first and second order, and sometimes of the third order. These kind of characters are especially to be named holy.

Whatsoever characters of this kind are to be instituted, we must draw about him a double circle, wherein we must write the name of his angel; and if we will add some divine name congruent with his spirit and office, it will be of greater force and efficacy; and if we draw about him any angular figure, according to the manner of his numbers that is lawful to be done. But the holy pictures which make the pentacles are they which every where are delivered to us in the prophets and sacred writings, both in the Old and New Testaments; even as the figure of the serpent hanging on the cross, and such like; whereof many may be found in the visions of the prophets, as in *Isaiah, Daniel, Esdras,* and others, and likewise in the revelations of the *Apocalypse.* And we have before spoken of them in our First Part, where we have made mention of holy things, therefore where any picture is posited of any of these holy images, let the circle be drawn round it on each side; wherein let there be written some divine name that is apt and conformed to the effect of that figure, or else there may be written around it some versicle taken out of part of the body of holy Scripture, which may ascertain or deprecate the desired effect.

If a pentacle were to be made to gain a victory, or revenge against one's enemies, as well visible as invisible, the figure may be taken out of the Second book of the *Maccabees;* that is to say, a hand holding a golden sword drawn, about which let there be written the versicle there contained, to wit, *take the holy sword, the gift of God, wherewith thou shalt slay the adversaries of my people Israel.* Or else there may be written about a versicle of the fifth Psalm; *in this is the strength of thy arm: before thy face there is death;* or some other such like versicle. But if you will write a divine name about the figure, then let some name be taken that signifies fear; a sword, wrath, the revenge of God, or some such like name congruent and agreeing with the effect desired. And if there shall be written any angular figure, let it be taken according to the rule of the numbers, as we have taught where we

BOOK II. have

have treated of numbers, and the like operations. And of this sort there are two pentacles of sublime virtue and great power, very useful and necessary to be used in the consecration of experiments and spirits; one whereof is that in the first chapter of the Apocalypse, to wit, a figure of the majesty of God sitting upon a throne, having in his mouth a two-edged sword, as there is described; about which let there be written, " I am Alpha and Omega, the Beginning and the End, which is, and which was, and which is to come, the Almighty. I am the First and the Last, who am living, and was dead, and behold I live for ever and ever; and I have the keys of death and hell." Then there shall be written about it these three versicles :

Munda Deus virtuti tuæ, &c.—Give commandment, O God, to thy strength; confirm, O God, thy strength in us. Let them be as dust before the face of the wind: and let the angel of the Lord scatter them. Let all their ways be darkness and uncertain: and let the angel of the Lord persecute them.

Moreover, let there be written about it the ten general names, which are *El, Elohim, Elohe, Zebaoth, Elion, Escerchie, Adonay, Jah, Tetragrammaton, Saday.*

There is another pentacle, the figure whereof is like *a lamb slain, having seven eyes and seven horns; and under his feet a book sealed with seven seals,* as it is in the fifth chapter of the *Apocalypse.* Round about let be written this versicle, *behold the lion hath overcome of the tribe of Judah, the root of David. I will open the book and unloose the seven seals thereof.* And another versicle, *I saw Satan like lightning fall down from heaven. Behold I have given you power to tread upon serpents and scorpions, and over all the power of your enemies, and nothing shall be able to hurt you.* And let there be also written about it the ten general names as aforesaid.

But those pentacles which are thus made of figures and names, let them keep this order; for when any figure is posited, conformable to any number, to produce any certain effect or virtue, there must be written thereupon, in all the several angles, some divine name obtaining the force and efficacy of the thing desired; yet so nevertheless, that the name which is of this sort do consist of just so many letters as the figure may constitute a number; or of so

many

many letters of a name, as, joined together among themselves, may make the number of a figure; or by any number which may be divided without any superfluity or diminution. Now such a name being found, whether it be only one name or more, or divers names, it is to be written in all the several angles in the figure; but in the middle of the figure let the revolution of the name be wholly and totally placed, or at least principally.

We likewise constitute pentacles by making the revolution of some kind of name, in a square table, and by drawing about it a single or double circle, and writing therein some holy versicle competent and befitting this name, or from which that name is extracted. And this is the way of making the pentacles, according to their several distinct forms and fashions, which we may, if we please, either multiply or commix together by course among themselves, to work the greater efficacy, extension and enlargement of force and virtue.

As, if a deprecation would be made for the overthrow and destruction of one's enemies, we are to mind, and call to remembrance how God destroyed the face of the whole earth in the deluge of waters, and the destruction of *Sodom* and *Gomorrah*, by raining down fire and brimstone; likewise, how God overthrew Pharaoh and his host in the Red Sea; and to call to mind if any other malediction or curse be found in holy writ. And thus in things of the like sort. So likewise in deprecating and praying against perils and dangers of waters, we ought to call to remembrance the saving of *Noah* in the deluge of waters, the passing of the children of *Israel* through the Red Sea; and also we are to mind how Christ walked on the waters, and how he saved the ship in danger from being cast away by the tempest; and how he commanded the winds and the waves, and they obeyed him; and also, that he drew *Peter* out of the water, being in danger of drowning, and the like. And, lastly, with these we invoke and call upon some certain holy names of God; to wit, such as are significative to accomplish our desire and accommodated to the desired effect; as if it be to overthrow enemies; we are to invoke and call upon names of *wrath, revenge, fear, justice,* and *fortitude* of God; and if we would avoid and

escape

escape any evil or danger, we then call upon the names of mercy, defence, salvation, fortitude, goodness, and such like names of God. When likewise we pray to God that he would grant us our desires, we are likewise to intermix therewith the name of some good spirit, whether one only, or more, whose office it is to execute our desires; and sometimes also we require some evil spirit to restrain or compel, whose name likewise we intermingle, and that rightly, especially if it be to execute any evil work; as *revenge, punishment,* or *destruction.*

Furthermore, if there be any versicle in the Psalms, or any other part of the holy Scripture, that shall seem congruent and agreeable to our desire, the same is to be mingled with our prayers. Now, after prayer has been made to God, it is expedient afterwards to make an oration to that executioner, whom, in our precedent prayer to God, we have desired should administer to us, whether one or more, or whether he be an angel, or star, or soul, or any of the noble angels. But this kind of oration ought to be composed according to the rules which we have delivered in the former part of our work, where we have treated of the manner of the composition of enchantments, *&c.*

You may know farther, that these kind of bonds have a threefold difference; for the first bond is when we conjure by natural things; the second is compounded of religious mysteries, by sacraments, miracles, and things of this sort; and the third is constituted by divine names and holy seals. With these kind of bonds we may bind not only spirits, but also other creatures whatsoever, as *animals, tempests, burnings, floods of waters, the force and power of arms.* Also we use these bonds aforesaid, not only by conjuration, but sometimes also using the means of deprecation and benediction. Moreover it conduces much to this purpose to join some sentence of holy Scripture, if any shall be found convenient thereto, as in the conjuration of serpents, by commemorating the curse of the serpent in the earthly paradise, and the setting up the serpent in the wilderness; and further, adding that versicle, *thou shalt walk upon the asp and the basilisk,* &c. Superstition is also of much prevelancy

lancy herein, by the translation of some sacramental rites, to bind that which we intend to hinder; as, the rites of excommunication, of sepulchres, funerals, buryings, and the like sort.

Of the Consecration of all magical Instruments and Materials which are used in this Art.

THE virtue of consecrations chiefly consists in two things, *viz.* the power of the person consecrating, and the virtue of the prayer by which the consecration is made.

For in the person consecrating, there is required firmness, constancy, and holiness of life; and that the consecrator himself shall, with a firm and undubitable faith, believe the virtue, power, and effect thereof.

Then in the prayer by which the consecration is made it derives its virtue either from divine inspiration, or else by composing it from sundry places in the holy Scriptures, in the commemoration of some of the wonderful miracles of God, effects, promises, sacraments and sacramental things, of which we have abundance in holy writ.

There must likewise be used the invocation of divine names, that are significative of the work in hand; likewise a sanctifying and expiation which is wrought by sprinkling with holy water, unctions with holy oil, and odoriferous suffumigations. Therefore in every consecration there is generally used a benediction and consecration of water, earth, oil, fire, and suffumigations, *&c.* with consecrated wax-lights or lamps burning; for without lights no consecration is duly performed. You must therefore particularly observe this, that when any thing (which we call prophane) is to be used, in which there is any defilement or pollution, it must, first of all, be purified by an *Exorcism* composed solely for that purpose, which ought to precede the consecration; which

which things being so made pure are most apt to receive the influences of the divine virtue. We must also observe that at the end of any consecration after the prayer is rightly performed, as we have mentioned, the operator ought to bless the thing consecrated, by breathing out some sentence with divine virtue and power of the present consecration, with a commemoration of his virtue and authority, that so it may be the more duly performed, and with an earnest and attentive mind. Now I shall mention here some examples, that, by these, a path may be made to the whole perfection thereof.

The Consecration of WATER.

SO in the consecration of water, we must commemorate that God has placed the firmament in the midst of the waters, and likewise that God placed the fountain of waters in the earthly paradise, from whence sprang four holy rivers that watered the whole earth; likewise we are to remember that God caused the waters to be an instrument of his justice in destroying the giants, by bringing on the deluge which covered the face of the whole earth; and in the overthrow of the host of Pharaoh in the Red Sea, and that God led the children of Israel through on dry land, and through the midst of the river Jordan, and likewise his marvellously drawing water out of the stony rock in the wilderness; and that, at the prayer of Samson, he caused water to flow out of the jaw-bone of an ass; and likewise that God has made water the instrument of his mercy and salvation for the expiation of original sin; also that Christ was baptized in the river Jordan, and hath thereby sanctified and cleansed the waters. Likewise certain divine names are to be invocated which are conformable hereto; as, that God is a living fountain, living water, the fountain of mercy, and names of the like sort.

Consecration

Consecration of FIRE.

AND likewise, in the consecration of fire, we are to commemorate that God hath created the fire to be an instrument to execute his justice, for punishment, vengeance, and the expiation of sins; also, when God comes to judge the world that he will command a conflagration of fire to go before him; likewise we are to mention that God appeared to Moses in a burning bush; and also how he went before the children of Israel in a pillar of fire; and that nothing can be duly offered, sanctified, or sacrificed, without fire; and how that God instituted fire to be kept in continually in the tabernacle of the covenant; and how miraculously he re-kindled the same, being extinct, and preserved it elsewhere from going out being hidden under the waters; and things of this sort; likewise the names of God are to be called upon which are consonant to this; as we read in the law and prophets, that God is a consuming fire; and likewise if there are any divine names which signify fire, as the glory of God, the light of God, the splendor and brightness of God, &c.

The Consecration of OIL.

AND likewise in the consecration of oil and perfumes we are to mention such things as are consonant to this purpose, as of the holy anointing oil mentioned in Exodus, and divine names significant thereunto; such as is the name Christ, which signifies *anointed;* and whatever mysteries there are relative to oil in the Scriptures, as the two olive-trees distilling holy oil into the lamps that burn before the face of God, mentioned in Revelations.

Of the Benediction of LIGHTS, LAMPS, WAX, &c.

NOW, the blessing of the lights, lamps, wax, &c. is taken from the fire, and whatever contains the substance of the flame, and whatever similitudes are in the mysteries, as the seven candlesticks which burn before the face of God.

Therefore

Therefore we have here given the manner of composing the consecrations, which first of all are necessary to be used in every kind of ceremony, and ought to precede every experiment or work, and without which nothing in magic rites can be duly performed.

In the next place, we will shew thee the consecration of *places*, *instruments*, and the like things.

The Consecration of PLACES, GROUND, CIRCLE, *&c.*

THEREFORE when you would consecrate any place or circle, you should take the prayer of Solomon used in the dedication and consecration of the temple; you must likewise bless the place by sprinkling with holy water and with suffumigations, and commemorate in the benediction holy mysteries; such as these, the sanctification of the throne of God, of Mount Sinai, of the tabernacle of the covenant, of the holy of holies, of the temple of Jerusalem: also the sanctification of Mount Golgotha, by the crucifixion of Christ; the sanctification of the temple of Christ; of Mount Tabor, by the transfiguration and ascension of Christ, *&c.* And by invocating all divine names which are significant to this; such as the place of God, the throne of God, the chair of God, the tabernacle of God, the altar of God, the habitation of God, and the like divine names of this sort, which are to be written about the circle, or place to be consecrated.

And, in the consecration of instruments, and every other thing that is used in this art, you must proceed after the same manner, by sprinkling with holy water the same, by fumigation, by anointing with holy oil, sealing it with some holy seal, and blessing it with prayer, and by commemorating holy things out of the sacred Scriptures, collecting divine names which are agreeable to the things to be consecrated; as for example, in the consecration of the sword we are to remember in the gospel, " he that hath two coats," *&c.* and that in the second of the Maccabees, it is said that a sword was divinely and miraculously sent to *Judas Maccabeus;* and if there is any thing of the like in the prophets, as " take unto you two-edged swords," *&c.* And you shall
also

also, in the same manner, consecrate experiments and books, and whatever of the like nature, as writings, pictures, &c. by sprinkling, perfuming, anointing, sealing, blessing, with holy commemorations, and call. 'g to remembrance the sanctification of mysteries ; as the table of the ten commandments, which were delivered to Moses by God in mount Sinai, the sanctification of the Old and New Testaments, and likewise of the law, prophets, and Scriptures, which were promulgated by the Holy Ghost : and again, there are to be mentioned such divine names as are convenient to this; as these are, *viz.* the testament of God, the book of God, the book of life, the knowledge of God, the wisdom of God, and the like. And with such kind of rites as these is the personal consecration performed.

There are beside these another rite of consecration of great power and efficacy; and this is one of the kinds of superstition, *viz.* when the rite of consecration or collection of any sacrament in the church is transferred to that thing which we would consecrate.

It must be noted that *vows*, *oblations*, and *sacrifices*, have the power of consecration also, as well real as personal ; and they are, as it were, certain conventions between those names with which they are made and us who make them, strongly cleaving to our desire and wished effects, as when we sacrifice with certain names, or things ; as fumigations, unctions, rings, images, mirrors ; and some things less material, as characters, seals, pentacles, enchantments, orations, pictures, Scriptures, of which we have largely spoken before.

Of the Invocation of EVIL SPIRITS, *and the binding of, and constraining of them to appear.*

NOW, if thou art desirous of binding any spirit to a ready obedience to thee, we will shew you how a certain book may be made by which they may be invoked ; and this book is to be consecrated a book of Evil Spirits, ceremoniously to be composed in their name and order, whereunto they bind

BOOK II.   with

with a certain holy oath, the ready and present obedience of the spirit. This book is therefore to be made of the most pure and clean paper, which is generally called virgin paper; and this book must be inscribed after this manner, *viz.* let there be drawn on the left side of the book the image of the spirit, and on the right side thereof his character, with the oath above it, containing the name of the spirit, his dignity and place, with his office and power. Yet many magicians do compose this book otherwise, omitting the characters and images; but I think that it is much more efficacious not to neglect any thing above mentioned in the forms.

There is likewise to be observed the circumstances of places, times, hours, according to the stars which these spirits are under, and are seen to agree to; with their site, rite, and order, being applied.

Which book being so written, is to be well bound, adorned, garnished, embellished and kept secure, with registers and seals, lest it should happen after the consecration to open in some part not designed, and endanger the operator. And, above all, let this book be kept as pure and reverent as possible; for irreverance of mind causes it to lose its virtue by pollution and prophanation.

Now this sacred book being thus composed according to the form and manner we have delivered, we are to consecrate it after a two-fold way; the first is, that all and singularly each of the spirits who are written in the book be called to the circle, according to the rites magical, which we have before taught, and place the book which is to be consecrated in a triangle on the outside of the circle; then read, in the presence of the spirits, all the oaths which are contained and written in that book; then the book to be consecrated being already placed without the circle in a triangle there drawn, compel all the spirits to impose their hands where their images and characters are drawn, and to confirm and consecrate the same with a special and common oath. This being done, let the book be shut and preserved as we have spoken before; then licence the spirits to depart according to due rite and magical order.

There

There is another method extant among us of consecrating a general book of spirits which is more easy, and of as much efficacy to produce every effect, except that in opening this book, the spirits do not always appear visible. And this way is thus : let be made a book of spirits, as we have before shewn, but in the end thereof write invocations, bonds, and strong conjurations, where-with every spirit may be bound ; then bind this book between two lamens or tables, and on the inside thereof draw or let be drawn two holy pentacles of the divine Majesty, which we have before set forth, out of the Apocalypse. Then let the first of them be placed in the beginning of the book, and the second at the end of the same.

This book being thus perfected, let it be brought, in a clear and fair night, to a circle prepared in a cross-way, according to the art which we have before delivered ; and there, in the first place, the book is to be opened, and to be consecrated according to the rites and ways which we have before delivered concerning consecration, which being done, let all the spirits be called which are written in the book, in their own order and place, conjuring them thrice by the bonds described in the book that they come to that place within the space of three days, to assure their obedience and confirm the same, to the book so to be consecrated ; then let the book be wrapped up in a clean linen cloth, and bury it in the midst of the circle, and stop the hole so as it may not be perceived or discovered : the circle being destroyed after you have licensed the spirits, depart before sun-rise ; and on the third day, about the middle of the night, return and make the circle anew and on thy knees make prayer unto God, and give thanks to him ; and let a precious perfume be made, open the hole in which you buried your book and take it out, and so let it be kept, not opening the same. Then after licensing the spirits in their order and destroying the circle, depart before sun-rise. And this is the last rite and manner of consecrating, profitable to what-ever writings, experiments, &c. that direct the spirits, placing the same between two holy lamens or pentacles, as is before mentioned.

But when the operator would work by the book thus consecrated he should do it in a fair and clear season, when the spirits are least troubled ; and let him

turn

turn himself towards the region of the spirits; then let him open the book under a due register, and likewise invoke the spirits by their oaths there described and confirmed, and by the name of their character and image, to whatever purpose you desire, and if there be need conjure them by the bonds placed
in the end of the book. *   And having attained thy desired effect license them
to depart.

And now we proceed to speak of the *Invocation of good as well as bad Spirits.*

The good spirits may be invoked of us, or by us, divers ways, and they in
sundry shapes and manners offer themselves to us, for they openly speak to those
that watch, and do offer themselves to our sight, or do inform us by dreams and
by oracle of those things which we have a great desire to know. Whoever therefore would call any good spirit to speak or appear in sight, he must particularly observe two things; one whereof is about the *disposition* of the invocant,
the other concerning those things which are outwardly to be adhibited
to the invocation for the conformity of the spirit to be called.

It is necessary therefore that the invocant religiously dispose himself for the
space of many days to such a mystery, and to conserve himself during the
time chaste, abstinent, and to abstract himself as much as he can from all manner of foreign and secular business; likewise he should observe fasting, as much
as shall seem convenient to him, and let him daily, between sun-rising and
setting, being clothed in pure white linen, seven times call upon God, and
make a deprecation to the angels to be called and invocated, according to the
rule which we have before taught. Now the number of days of fasting and
preparation is commonly one month, *i. e.* the time of a whole lunation. Now,
in the Cabala, we generally prepare ourselves forty days before.

Now concerning the place, it must be chosen clean, pure, close, quiet, free
from all manner of noise, and not subject to any stranger's sight. This place
must first of all be exorcised and consecrated; and let there be a table or altar
placed therein, covered with a clean white linen cloth, and set towards the
east: and on each side thereof place two consecrated wax-lights burning, the

* I have given an example of the book of spirits, by which you may see the method in which the
characters, &c. are placed as above described. See the Plate.

flame

flame thereof ought not to go out all these days.   In the middle of the altar
let there be placed lamens, or the holy paper we have before described, covered with fine linen, which is not to be opened until the end of the days of
consecration.   You shall also have in readiness a *precious perfume* and a *pure
anointing oil.*—And let them both be kept consecrated.   Then set a sensor on
the head of the altar, wherein you shalt kindle the *holy fire*, and make a precious perfume every day that you pray.

Now for your habit, you shall have a long garment of white linen, close before and behind, which may come down quite over the feet, and gird yourself
about the loins with a girdle.   You shall likewise have a veil made of pure
white linen on which must be wrote in a gilt lamen, the name *Tetragrammaton ;*
all which things are to be consecrated and sanctified in order.   But you
must not go into this holy place till it be first washed and covered with a cloth
new and clean, and then you may enter, but with your feet naked and bare ;
and when you enter therein you shall sprinkle with holy water, then make a
perfume upon the altar ; and then on thy knees pray before the altar as we
have directed.

Now when the time is expired, on the last day, you shall fast more strictly ;
and fasting on the day following, at the rising of the sun, enter the holy place,
using the ceremonies before spoken of, first by sprinkling thyself, then, making
a perfume, you shall sign the cross with holy oil in the forehead, and anoint
your eyes, using prayer in all these consecrations.   Then, open the lamen and
pray before the altar upon your knees ; and then an invocation may be made as
follows :

An INVOCATION *of the* GOOD SPIRITS.

IN the name of the blessed and Holy Trinity, I do desire thee, strong
and mighty angels (*here name the spirits you would have appear*) that if it be
the divine will of him who is called Tetragrammaton, *&c.* the holy God, the
Father, that thou take upon thee some shape as best becometh thy celestial
nature, and appear to us visibly here in this place, and answer our demands, in
as far as we shall not transgress the bounds of the divine mercy and goodness,

by

by requesting unlawful knowledge; but that thou wilt graciously shew us what things are most profitable for us to know and do to the glory and honour of his divine Majesty who liveth and reigneth, world without end. *Amen.*

Lord thy will be done on earth as it is in heaven—make clean our hearts within us, and take not thy holy spirit from us. O Lord, by thy name we have called them, suffer them to administer unto us.

And that all things may work together for thy honour and glory, to whom with thee, the Son and blessed Spirit, be ascribed all might, majesty, and dominion world without end. *Amen.*

The particular Form of the LAMEN.—(For the form of the Lamen see the. Plate.)

THE invocation being made, the good angels will appear unto you which you desire, which you shall entertain with a chaste communication, and licence them to depart.

Now the lamen which is used to invoke any good spirit must be made after the following manner: either in metal conformable or in new wax mixed with convenient spices and colours; or it may be made with pure white paper with convenient colours, and the outward form of it may be either square, circular, or triangular, or of the like sort, according to the rule of the numbers, in which there must be written the divine names, as well general as special. And in the centre of the lamen draw a hexagon or character of six corners, in the middle thereof write the name and character of the star, or of the spirit his governor, to whom the good spirit that is to be called is subject. And about this character let there be placed so many characters of five corners or pentacles as the spirits we would call together at once. But if we should call only one, nevertheless there must be made four pentagons, wherein the name of the spirit or spirits, with their characters, are to be written. Now this lamen ought to be composed when the moon is in her increase, on those days and hours which agree to the spirit; and if we take a fortunate planet therewith,

therewith, it will be the better for the producing the effect : which table or lamen being rightly made in the manner we have fully described, must be consecrated according to the rules above delivered.

And this is the way of making the general table or lamen for the invocating of all spirits whatever; the form whereof you may see in the Plates of pentacles, seals, and lamens.

Nevertheless, we make special tables congruent to every spirit by the rule which we have above spoken concerning holy pentacles.

We will yet declare unto you another rite more easy to perform this thing : let the man who wishes to receive an oracle from a spirit be chaste, pure, and sanctified; then a place being chosen pure, clean, and covered every where with clean and white linen, on the Lord's-day in the new of the moon, let him enter into that place clothed with white linen; let him exorcise the place, bless it, and make a circle therein with a consecrated coal; let there be written in the outer part of the circle the names of the angels; in the inner part thereof write the mighty names of God; and let be placed within the circle, at the four parts of the world, the vessels for the perfumes. Then, being washed and fasting, let him enter the place and pray towards the east this whole Psalm, " Blessed are the undefiled in the way," &c. Psalm cxix. Then make a fumigation, and deprecate the angels by the said divine names, that they will appear unto you, and reveal or discover that which you so earnestly desire; and do this continually for six days, washed and fasting. On the seventh day, being washed and fasting, enter the circle, perfume it, and anoint thyself with holy oil upon the forehead, eyes, and in the palms of both hands, and upon the feet; then, with bended knees, say the Psalm aforesaid, with divine and angelical names. Which being said, arise, and walk round the circle from *East* to *West*, until thou shalt be wearied with a giddiness of thy head and brain, then straitway fall down in the circle, where thou mayest rest, and thou wilt be wrapped up in an ecstasy; and a spirit will appear and inform thee of all things necessary to be known. We must observe also, that in the circle there ought to be four holy candles
burning

burning at the four parts of the world, which ought not to want light for the
space of a week.

And the manner of fasting is this : to abstain from all things having a life
of sense, and from those which do proceed from them, let him drink only
pure running water; neither is there any food or wine to be taken till the going
down of the sun.

Let the perfume and the holy anointing oil be made as is set forth in
Exodus, and other holy books of the Bible. It is also to be observed, that
as often as he enters the circle he has upon his forehead a golden lamen,
upon which there must be written the name *Tetragrammaton,* in the manner
we have before mentioned.

Of ORACLES *by* DREAMS.

BUT natural things and their own commixtures do likewise belong unto
magicians, and we often use such to receive oracles from a spirit by a dream;
which are either by perfumes, unctions, meats, drinks, seals, rings, *&c.*

Now those who are desirous to receive oracles in or through a dream,
let him make himself a ring of the sun or Saturn for this purpose. There
are likewise images of dreams, which, being put under the head when he
goes to sleep, doth effectually give true dreams of whatever the mind
hath before determined or consulted upon, the practice of which is as
follows :

Thou shalt make an image of the sun, the figure whereof must be, a
man sleeping upon the bosom of an angel, which thou shalt make when Leo
ascends, the sun being in the ninth house in Aries; thou shalt write upon the
figure the name of the effect desired, and in the hand of the angel the name
of the intelligence of the sun. Let the same image be made in Virgo
ascending, Mercury being fortunate in Aries in the ninth; or Gemini ascending, Mercury being fortunate in the ninth house in Aquarius; and let

it

it be received with Saturn with a fortunate aspect, and let the name of the spirit be written upon it. Let the same likewise be made in Libra ascending, Venus being received from Mercury in Gemini in the ninth house, and write upon it the angel of Venus. Again, you may make the same image Aquarius ascending, Saturn fortunately possessing the ninth in his exaltation, which is Libra; and let there be written upon it the angel of Saturn. The same may be made Cancer ascending, the moon being received by Jupiter and Venus in Pisces, and being fortunately placed in the ninth house, and write upon it the spirit of the moon.

There are likewise made rings of dreams of wonderful efficacy; and there are rings of the sun and Saturn; and the constellation of them is when the sun or Saturn ascend in their exaltations in the ninth, and when the moon is joined to Saturn in the ninth, and in that sign which was the ninth house of the nativity; and write and engrave upon the rings the name of the spirit of the sun or Saturn; and by these rules you may know how and by what means to constitute more of thyself: but know this, that such images work nothing (as they are simply images) unless they are vivified by a spiritual and celestial virtue, and chiefly by the ardent desire and firm intent of the soul of the operator. But who can give a soul to an image, or make a stone, or metal, or clay, or wood, or wax, or paper to live? certainly no man; (for this arcanum doth not enter into an artist of a stiff neck,) he only hath it who transcends the progress of angels, and comes to the very architype himself.

The tables of numbers likewise confer to the receiving of oracles, being duly formed under their own constellations. Holy tables and papers likewise serve to this effect, being especially composed and consecrated; such as the *Almutel* of *Solomon*, and the Table of the Revolution of the name *Tetragrammaton;* and those things which are of this kind, and written to produce these effects, out of various figures, numbers, holy Scriptures, and pictures, with inscriptions of the divine names of God and names of holy angels; the composition whereof is taken out of diverse places of the holy Scriptures, Psalms, and versicles, and other certain promises out of the divine revelations and prophecies.

Book II.   To

To the same effect do conduce, likewise, holy prayers and deprecations as well to God as to the blessed angels ; the deprecations of which prayers are to be composed, as we have before shewn, according to some religious similitude, making mention of those things which we intend to do ; as out of the Old Testament of the dream of Jacob, Joseph, Pharaoh, Daniel, and Nebuchadnezzar : if out of the New Testament, of the dream of Joseph ; of the three wise men, or magi, of John the evangelist sleeping upon the breast of our Lord ; and whatever of the like kind can be found in religion, miracles, and revelation. According to which the deprecation may be composed ; if when he goes to sleep it be with a firm intention, and then, without doubt, they will afford a wonderful effect.

Therefore he who is desirous of receiving true oracles by dreams, let him abstain from supper, from drink, and be otherwise well disposed, so his brain will be free from turbulent vapours ; let him also have his bed-chamber fair and clean, *exorcised* and *consecrated* if he will ; then let him perfume the same with some convenient fumigation, and let him anoint his temples with some unguent efficacious hereunto, and put a ring of dreams upon his finger ; then let him take one of the images we have spoken of, or some holy table, or paper, and place the same under his head ; then, having 'made a devout prayer, let him address himself to sleep, meditating upon that thing which he desires to know ; so shall he receive a most certain and undoubted oracle by a dream, when the moon goes through that sign which was in the ninth house of his nativity, and also when she goes through the sign of the ninth of the revolution of his nativity, and when she is in the ninth sign from the sign of perfection.

This is the way whereby we may obtain all sciences and arts whatsoever, whether alchemy, magic, or else, suddenly and perfectly with a true illumination of our intellect ; although all inferior familiar spirits whatsoever conduce to this effect, and sometimes also evil spirits sensibly inform us intrinsically and extrinsically.

Of

Of the Method of raising EVIL *or* FAMILIAR SPIRITS *by a* CIRCLE; *likewise the Souls and Shadows of the Dead.*

IT is here convenient that we say something about the means used by exorcists to raise up what are usually termed evil spirits to the circle, and the methods of calling up the ghosts or souls of those who have died a violent or premature death.

Now, if any one would call any evil spirit to the circle, he must first consider and know his nature, and to which of the planets it agrees, and what offices are distributed unto him from the planet. This being known, let there be sought out a place fit and convenient, and proper for his invocation, according to the nature of the planet and the quality of the offices of the same spirit, as near as it can be done; as if their power be over the sea, rivers or floods, then let the place be the sea-shore, and so of the rest. Then chuse a convenient time both for the quality of the air (being serene, quiet, clear and fitting for the spirits to assume bodies); as also of the quality of and nature of the planet and the spirit, as on his day and time in which he rules; he may be fortunate or unfortunate sometimes of the day, and sometimes of the night, as the stars and spirits do require.

These things being judiciously considered, let the circle be made at the place elected, as well for the defence of the invocant as the confirmation of the spirit. And in the circle write the divine general names, and all those things which do yield defence to us; and, with them, those divine names which do rule his planet, and the offices of the spirit himself; likewise write therein the names of the good spirits which bear rule in the time you do this, and are able to bind and constrain that spirit which we intend to call. And if we will further strengthen and fortify our circle, we may add characters and pentacles agreeing to the work; then also, if we will, we may either, within or without the circle, frame an angular figure with the inscription of such convenient numbers as are congruent amongst themselves to our work, which

are

are to be known according to the manner of numbers and figures delivered in our first Book.

Further we are to be provided with *lights*, perfumes, unguents, and medicines, compounded according to the nature of the spirit and planet which agree with the spirit by reason of their natural and celestial virtue.

Then we are to be furnished with holy and consecrated things necessary, not only for the defence of the invocant and his companions, but also serving for bonds to bind and constrain the spirits; such as holy papers, lamens, pictures, pentacles, swords, scepters, garments of convenient colour and matter.

Then, with all these things provided, let the exorcist and his companions go into the circle. In the first place, let him consecrate the circle and every thing he uses; which being done in a solemn and firm manner, with convenient gesture and countenance, let him begin to pray with a loud voice after the manner following. First, by making an oration or prayer to God, and then intreating the good spirits; but we should read some prayer, or psalm, or gospel, for our defence in the first place. After those prayers and orations are said, let him begin to invocate the spirit which he desireth, with a gentle and loving enchantment to all the coasts of the world, with a commemoration of his own authority and power. Then rest and look round to see if any spirit does appear; which if he delays, then let him repeat his invocation, as above said, until he hath done it three times; and if the spirit is obstinate and will not appear, then let the invocator begin to *conjure* him with divine power; but so that all his conjurations and commemorations do agree with the nature and office of the spirit, and reiterate the same three times, from stronger to stronger, using contumelies, cursings, punishments, suspension from his power and office, and the like.

And after these courses are finished, cease; and if the spirit shall appear, let the invocant turn himself towards the spirit, and courteously receive him, and, earnestly entreating him, let him ask his name, which write down on your holy paper, and then proceed by asking him whatsoever you will; and if in any

thing

thing the spirit shall appear to be *obstinate, ambiguous,* or *lying,* let him be bound by convenient conjurations; and if you doubt any thing, make, without the circle with the consecrated sword, the figure of a triangle or pentagon, and compel the spirit to enter into it; and if you receive any promise which you would have confirmed with an oath, stretch the sword out of the circle, and swear the spirit by laying his hand on the sword. Then having obtained of the spirit that which you desire, or are otherwise contented, license him to depart with courteous words, giving command that he do no hurt; and if he will not depart, compel him by powerful conjurations; and if need require expel him by exorcisms and by making contrary suffumigations. And when he is departed, go not out of the circle, but make a stay, and use some prayer giving thanks to God and the good angels; and also praying for your future defence and conservation, which being orderly performed you may depart.

But if your hopes are frustrated, and no spirit will appear, yet for this you need not despair; but leaving the circle after licensing to depart (*which must never be omitted whether a spirit appears or not* *,) return at other times, doing as before. And if you think that you have erred in any thing, then you shall amend by adding or diminishing; for the constancy of repetition encreases your authority and power, and strikes a terror into the spirits, and compels them to obey.

And often the spirits do come although they appear not visible (to cause terror to him who calls them,) either in the thing which he uses, or else in the operation itself. But this kind of licensing is not given *simply,* but by a kind of dispensation, with suspension, until they shall render themselves obedient: also, without a circle, these spirits may be called to appear, by the way we have delivered in the consecration of a book. But when we intend to execute any effect where an apparition is not needful, then that is to be done, by making and forming that which is to be to us an instrument; as whether it be an image, ring, character, table, writing, candle, sacrifice, or

---

* They who neglect licensing the spirits are in very great danger, because instances have been known of the operator experiencing sudden death.

any

any thing else; then the name of the spirit is to be written therein with his character, according to the exigency of the experiment, either by writing it with blood, or otherwise using a perfume agreeable to the spirit. Likewise we are often to make orations and prayers to God and the good angels before we invocate any evil spirit, conjuring him by divine power.

In some former parts of our work we have taught how and by what means the soul is joined to the body.

We will in this place inform thee farther, that those souls do still love their relinquished bodies after death, a certain affinity alluring them as it were. Such are the souls of noxious men who have violently relinquished their bodies, and souls wanting a due burial, which still wander in a liquid and turbulent spirit about their dead carcasses; but these souls, by the known means by which they were joined to their bodies, by the like vapours, liquors, and savours, are easily drawn into them.

Hence it is that the souls of the dead are not to be called up without blood or by the application of some part of their relict body.

In the *raising* therefore of these shadows, we are to perfume with new blood the bones of the dead, and with flesh, eggs, milk, honey, and oil, which furnish the soul with a medium apt to receive its body.

It is likewise to be understood, those who are desirous to raise any souls of the dead, ought to select those places wherein these kind of souls are most known to be conversant; or by some alliance alluring the souls into their forsaken *bodies*, or by some kind of affection in times past impressed in them in their life, drawing the souls to certain places, things, or persons; or by the forcible nature of some place fitted and prepared to purge or punish these souls : which places for the most part, are to be known by the appearance of visions, nightly incursions, and apparitions.

Therefore the places most fitting for these things are church-yards. And better than them are those places devoted to the executions of criminal judg- ments; and better than these are those places where, of late years, there have been so great and so many public slaughters of men; and that place is still better than those where some dead carcass that came by violent death is

not

not yet expiated, nor was lately buried ; for the expiation of those places is likewise a holy rite duly to be adhibited to the burial of the bodies, and often prohibits the soul returning to its body, and expels the same afar off to the place of judgment.

And from hence it is that the souls of the dead are not easy to be raised up, except it be the souls of them whom we know to be evil, or to have perished by a violent death, and whose bodies do want the rite of due burial.

Now although we have spoken concerning such places of this kind, it will not be safe or commodious to go unto them ; but it is requisite for us to take to whatsoever place is to be chosen some principal relict of the body, and therewith make a perfume in due manner, and to perform other competent rites.

It is also to be known, that because the souls are certain spiritual lights, therefore artificial lights framed out of certain competent things, compounded according to a true rule, with congruent inscriptions of names and seals, do very much avail to the raising up of departed souls.   But those things which are now spoken of are not always sufficient to raise up souls, because of an extra-natural portion of understanding and reason, which is above and known only to the heavenly destinies and their powers.

We should therefore allure the said souls by supernatural and celestial powers duly administered, even by those things which do move the very harmony of the soul, as well imaginative as rational and intellectual, such as voices, songs, sounds, enchantments ; and religious things, as prayers, conjurations, exorcisms, and other holy rites, which may commodiously be administered hereunto.

END OF PART SECOND.

A Table, shewing the names of the Angels governing the 7 days of the week, with their Sigils, Planets, Signs, &c.

Sunday	Monday	Tuesday	Wednesday	Thursday	Friday	Saturday
Michaël	Gabriel	Camael	Raphaël	Sachiel	Ana'el	Cassiel
name of their Heaven	name of the Heaven	name of the Heaven	name of the Heaven	name of their Heaven	name of their Heaven	is Angels ruling above the 6th Heaven
Machen.	Shamain.	Machon.	Raquie.	Zebul.	Sagun.	

A specimen of the Book of Spirits to be made of virgin Vellum.

The Book of Spirits

Saturday ♄   Cassiel Ruler

Cassiel

PARTICULAR COMPOSITION

MAGICAL CIRCLE;

OF

EXORCISMS, BENEDICTIONS, AND THE CONJURATIONS OF EVERY DAY IN THE WEEK;

AND

THE MANNER OF WORKING DESCRIBED.

BOOK II. PART III.

THE following instructions are the principal and sum total of all we have said, only we have brought it rather into a closer train of experiment and practice than any of the rest; for here you may behold the distinct functions of the spirits; likewise the whole perfection of magical ceremonies is here described, syllable by syllable.

But as the greatest power is attributed to the circles, (for they are certain fortresses,) we will now clearly explain, and shew the composition and figure of a circle.

The Composition of the CIRCLE.—(For the figure of the Circle see the Plate.)

The forms of circles are not always one and the same, but are changed according to the order of spirits that are to be called, their places, times,

days,

days, and hours ; for in making a circle it ought to be considered in what time of the year, what day, and what hour, what spirits you would call, and to what star or region they belong, and what functions they have : therefore, to begin, let there be made three circles of the latitude of nine feet, distant one from another about a hand's breadth. First, write in the middle circle *the name of the hour* wherein you do the work; in the second place, write *the name of the angel of the hour*; in the third place, the seal of the angel of the hour; fourthly, the name of the angel that rules the day in which you work, and the names of his ministers ; in the fifth place, the name of the present time ; sixthly, the name of the spirits ruling in that part of time, and their *presidents*; seventhly, the name of the head of the sign ruling in the time ; eighthly, the name of the earth, according to the time of working ; ninthly, and for the compleating of the middle circle, write the name of the sun and moon, according to the said rule of time : for as the times are changed, so are the names : and in the outer circle let there be drawn, in the four angles, the names of the great presidential spirits of the air that day wherein you would do this work, *viz.* the name of the king and his three ministers. Without the circle, in four angles, let *pentagons* be made. In the inner circle write four divine names, with four crosses interposed : in the middle of the circle, *viz.* towards the east let be written Alpha ; towards the west, Omega ; and let a cross divide the middle of the circle.

When the circle is thus finished, according to rule, you shall proceed to consecrate and bless it, saying,

In the name of the holy, blessed, and glorious Trinity, proceed we to our work in these mysteries to accomplish that which we desire ; we therefore, in the names aforesaid, consecrate this piece of ground for our defence, so that no spirit whatsoever shall be able to break these boundaries, neither be able to cause injury nor detriment to any of us here assembled ; but that they may be compelled to stand before this circle, and answer truly our demands, so far as it pleaseth Him who liveth for ever and ever ; and who says, I am Alpha and Omega, the Beginning and the End, which is, and which was, and which is to come, the Almighty ; I am the First and the Last, who am living and was dead ; and behold I live

for

The
Magic
Circle

Veacan Rex

Yaya Michael

Al·pha.

TETRAGRAMATON

et ω

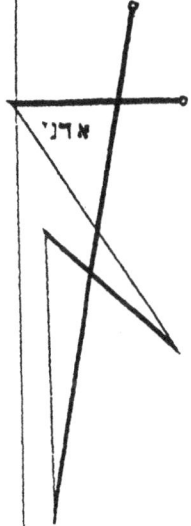

אדני

Magic Ring

The
Lemon

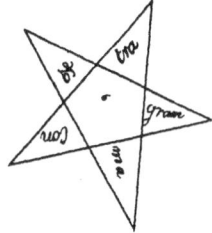

The Pentacle of
Solomon

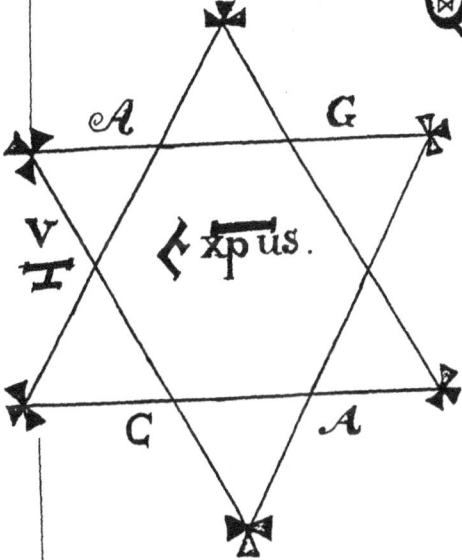

A   G

Xpus.

V
H

C   A

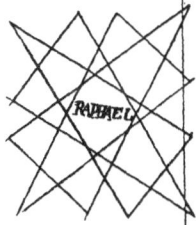

RAPHAEL

There is no poison
to the Magical
Wand

for ever and ever ; and I have the keys of death and hell.   Bless, O Lord !
this creature of earth wherein we stand ; confirm, O God ! thy strength in us, so
that neither the adversary nor any evil thing may cause us to fail, through the
merits of Jesus Christ.   Amen.

It is also to be known that the angels rule the hours in a successive order,
according to the course of the heavens and the planets to which they are subject ; so the same spirit which governeth the day rules also the first hour of the
day ; the second from this governs the second hour, and so on throughout ;
and when seven planets and hours have made their revolution it returns again
to the first which rules the day.   Therefore we shall first speak of the names of
the hours, *viz.*

A Table *shewing the* Magical Names *of the* Hours, *both* Day
and Night.

	Names of Hours of the Day.		Names of Hours of the Night.
1	Yain	1	Beron
2	Janor	2	Barol
3	Nasnia	3	Thami
4	Salla	4	Athar
5	Sadedali	5	Methon
6	Thamur	6	Rana
7	Ourer	7	Netos
8	Thamic	8	Tafrac
9	Neron	9	Sassur
10	Jayon	10	Agle
11	Abai	11	Calerva
12	Natalon	12	Salam

Of the names of the angels and their seals it shall be spoken in their proper
places ; but here we will shew the names of the times.

A year

A year therefore is four-fold, and is divided into spring, summer, autumn, and winter ; the names thereof are these :

The spring, *Talvi* ; the summer, *Casmaran* ; autumn, *Adarcel* ; winter, *Farlas*.

The ANGELS *of the* SPRING—Caracasa, Core, Amatiel, Commissoros.

The head of the sign in spring is called Spugliguel.

The name of the earth in spring, Amadai.

The names of the sun and moon in spring : sun, Abraym ; moon, Agusita.

The ANGELS *of the* SUMMER—Gargatel, Tariel, Gaviel.

The head of the sign of the summer, Tubiel.

The name of the earth in summer, Festativi.

The names of the sun and moon in summer : sun, Athemay ; moon, Armatus.

The ANGELS *of the* AUTUMN—Tarquam, Guabarel.

The head of the sign of autumn, Torquaret.

The name of the earth in autumn, Rabinnara.

The names of the sun and moon in autumn : the sun, Abragini ; the moon, Matasignais.

The ANGELS *of the* WINTER—Amabael, Cetarari.

The head of the sign of winter, Attarib.

The name of the earth in winter, Geremiah.

The names of the sun and moon in winter : the sun, Commutoff ; the moon, Affaterim.

These things being known, finish the consecration of the circle by saying,

" Thou shalt purge me with hysop, O Lord, and I shall be clean : thou shalt wash me and I shall be whiter than snow."

Then sprinkle the same with holy water, and proceed with the benediction of the perfumes.

BENE-

BENEDICTION *of* PERFUMES.

THE God of Abraham, God of Isaac, God of Jacob, bless here the creatures of these kinds, that they may fill up the power and virtue of their odours; so that neither the enemy nor any false imagination may be able to enter into them; through our Lord Jesus Christ, *&c.* Then sprinkle the same with holy water.

The EXORCISM *of* FIRE *into which the* PERFUMES *are to be put.*

I EXORCISE thee, O thou creature of fire, by the only true God Jehovah, Adonai, Tetragrammaton, that forthwith thou cast away every phantasm from thee, that it shall do no hurt to any one. We beseech thee, O Lord, to bless this creature of fire, and sanctify it, so that it may be blessed to set forth the praise and glory of thy holy name, and that no hurt may be permitted to come to the exorciser or spectators; through our Lord Jesus Christ. *Amen.*

Of the HABIT *of the* EXORCIST.

IT should be made, as we have before described, of fine white linen and clean, and to come round the body loose, but close before and behind.

Of the PENTACLE *of* SOLOMON.—(For the fig. see the Plate.)

IT is always necessary to have this pentacle in readiness to bind with, in case the spirits should refuse to be obedient, as they can have no power over the exorcist while provided with and fortified by the pentacle, the virtue of the holy names therein written presiding with wonderful influence over the spirits.

It should be made in the day and hour of Mercury upon parchment made of a kidskin, or virgin, or pure, clean, white paper; and the figures and

letters

letters wrote in pure gold; and it ought to be consecrated and sprinkled (as before often spoken) with holy water.

When the vesture is put on, it will be convenient to say the following oration:

An ORATION *when the* HABIT *or* VESTURE *is put on.*

ANOOR, Amacor, Amides, Theodonias, Anitor; by the merits of the angels, O Lord! I will put on the garment of salvation, that this which I desire I may bring to effect, through thee, the most holy Adonai, whose kingdom endureth for ever and ever. *Amen.*

The Manner of Working.

LET the moon be increasing and equal, if it can then be conveniently done; but especially let her not be combust, or in Via Combusta, which is between fourteen degrees of Libra and fourteen degrees of Scorpio.

The operator ought to be clean and purified for nine days before he does the work. Let him have ready the perfume appropriated to the day wherein he does the work; and he must be provided with holy water from a clergyman, or he may make it holy himself, by reading over it the consecration of water of baptism; he must have a new vessel of earth, with fire, the vesture, and the pentacle; and let all these things be rightly and duly consecrated and prepared. Let one of the companions carry the vessel with fire, and the perfumes, and let another bear the book, the garment, and pentacle; and let the operator himself carry the sword, over which should be said a prayer of consecration: and on the middle of the sword on one side let there be engraven *Agla* †, and on the other side, † *On,* † Tetragrammaton †. And the place being fixed upon where the circle is to be erected, let him draw the lines we have before taught, and sprinkle the same with holy water, consecrating, &c. &c.

The

The operator ought therefore to be prepared with fasting, chastity, and abstinence, for the space of three days before the day of operation; and on the day that he would do this work, being clothed with the fore-mentioned vesture, and furnished with *pentacles, perfumes,* a *sword, bible, paper, pen,* and *consecrated ink,* and *all things necessary hereunto,* let him enter the circle, and call the angels from the four parts of the world which do rule the seven planets, the seven days of the week, colours, and metals, whose names you will see in their places; and, with bended knees, first let him say the Paternoster or Lord's Prayer, and then let him invocate the said angels, saying,

O angeli! supradicti estote adiutores mihi petitioni & in adjutorum mihi, in meis rebus et petitionibus.

Then call the angels from the four parts of the world that rule the air the same day in which he makes the experiment; and, having employed especially all the names and spirits within the circle, say,

O vos omnes, adjutore atque contestor per sedem Adonai, per Hagios, Theos, Ischyros, Athanatos, Paracletos, Alpha & Omega, & per hæc tria nomina secreta, Agla, On, Tetragrammaton, quod hodie debeatis adimplere quod cupio.

These things being performed, let him read the conjuration assigned for the day; but if they shall be pertinacious or refractory, and will not yield themselves obedient, neither to the conjuration assigned for the day, nor any of the prayers before made, then use the exorcism following:

A GENERAL EXORCISM *of the* SPIRITS *of the* AIR.

WE being made after the image of God, endued with power from God and made after his will, do exorcise you, by the most mighty and powerful name of God, *El,* strong and wonderful, *(here name the spirit which is to appear,)* and we command you by Him who spoke the word and it was done, and by all the names of God, and by the name Adonai, El, Elohim, Elohe, Zebaoth, Elion, Eserchie, Jah, Tetragrammaton, Sadai, Lord God Most High: we exorcise you, and powerfully command you that you forthwith appear unto us here before this circle in a fair human shape, without any deformity
mity

mity or tortuosity; come ye all such, because we command you by the name Yaw and Vau, which Adam heard and spoke; and by the name of God, Agla, which Lot heard, and was saved with his family; and by the name Joth, which Jacob heard from the angel wrestling with him, and was delivered from the hand of his brother Esau; and by the name Anaphexeton, which Aaron heard and spoke, and was made wise; and by the name Zebaoth, which Moses named, and all the rivers were turned into blood; and by the name Eserchie Oriston, which Moses named, and all the rivers brought forth frogs, and they ascended into the houses of the Egyptians, destroying all things; and by the name Elion, which Moses named, and there was great hail, such as had not been since the beginning of the world; and by the name Adonai, which Moses named, and there came up locusts, which appeared upon the whole land of Egypt, and devoured all which the hail had left; and by the name Schema Amathia, which Joshua called upon, and the sun stayed his course; and by the name Alpha and Omega, which Daniel named, and destroyed Bel and slew the dragon; and in the name Emmanuel, which the three children, Sidrach, Misach, and Abednego, sung in the midst of the fiery furnace, and were delivered; and by the name Hagios; and by the seal of Adonai; and by Ischyros, Athanatos, Paracletos; and by these three secret names, Agla, On, Tetragrammaton, I do adjure and contest you; and by these names, and by all the other names of the living and true God, our Lord Almighty, I exorcise and command you, by Him who spoke the word and it was done, to whom all creatures are obedient; and by the dreadful judgment of God; and by the uncertain sea of glass, which is before the divine *Majesty*, mighty and powerful; by the four beasts before the throne, having eyes before and behind; and by the fire round about his throne; and by the holy angels of heaven; by the mighty wisdom of God, we do powerfully exorcise you, that you appear here before this circle, to fulfil our will in all things which shall seem good unto us; by the seal of Baldachia, and by this name Primeumaton, which *Moses* named, and the earth opened and swallowed up Corah, Dathan, and Abiram: and in the power of that name Primeumaton, commanding the whole host of heaven, we curse you, and deprive you of your

office,

office, joy, and place, and do bind you in the depth of the bottomless pit, there to remain until the dreadful day of the last judgment; and we bind you into eternal fire, and into the lake of fire and brimstone, unless you forthwith appear before this circle to do our will : therefore, come ye, by these names, Adonai, Zebaoth, Adonai, Amioram; come ye, come ye, come ye, Adonai commandeth; Saday, the most mighty King of Kings, whose power no creature is able to resist, be unto you most dreadful, unless ye obey, and forthwith affably appear before this circle, let miserable ruin and fire unquenchable remain with you; therefore come ye, in the name of Adonai, Zebaoth, Adonai, Amioram; come, come, why stay you? hasten! Adonai, Sadai, the King of Kings commands you : El, Aty, Titcip, Azia, Hin, Jen, Minosel, Achadan, Vay, Vaah, Ey, Exe, A, El, El, El, A, Hy, Hau, Hau, Hau, Vau, Vau, Vau, Vau.

A PRAYER *to* GOD, *to be said in the four Parts of the* WORLD *in the* CIRCLE.·

AMORULE, Taneha, Latisten, Rabur, Teneba, Latisten, Escha, Aladia, Alpha and Omega, Leyste, Orision, Adonai; O most merciful heavenly Father! have mercy upon me, although a sinner; make appear the arm of thy power in me this day against these obstinate spirits, that I, by thy will, may be made a contemplator of thy divine works, and may be illustrated with all wisdom, to the honour and glory of thy holy name. I humbly beseech thee, that these spirits which I call by thy judgment may be bound and constrained to come and give true and perfect answers to those things which I shall ask of them; and that they may do and declare those things unto us, which by me may be commanded of them, not hurting any creature, neither injuring or terrifying me or my fellows, nor hurting any other creature, and affrighting no man; and let them be obedient to those things which are required of them.

Then

Then, standing in the middle of the circle, stretch out thy hand towards the pentacle, saying, *By the pentacle of Solomon I have called you; give me a true answer.*

Then follows this ORATION.

BERALANENSIS, Baldachiensis, Paumachia, and Apologia Sedes, by the most mighty kings and powers, and the most powerful princes, genii, Liachidæ, ministers of the Tartarean seat, chief prince of the seat of Apologia, in the ninth legion, I invoke you, and by invocating, conjure you; and being armed with power from the supreme Majesty, I strongly command you, by Him who spoke and it was done, and to whom all creatures are obedient; and by this ineffable name, Tetragrammaton Jehovah, which being heard the elements are overthrown, the air is shaken, the sea runneth back, the fire is quenched, the earth trembles, and all the host of the celestials, and terrestrials, and infernals do tremble together, and are troubled and confounded : wherefore, forthwith and without delay, do you come from all parts of the world, and make rational answers unto all things I shall ask of you; and come ye peaceably, visibly and affably now, without delay, manifesting what we desire, being conjured by the name of the living and true God, Helioren, and fulfil our commands, and persist unto the end, and according to our intentions, visibly and affably speaking unto us with a clear voice, intelligible, and without any ambiguity.

Of the APPEARANCE *of the* SPIRITS.

THESE things being duly performed, there will appear infinite visions, apparitions, phantasms, *&c.* beating of drums, and the sound of all kinds of musical instruments; which is done by the spirits, that with the terror they might force some of the companions out of the circle, because they can effect nothing against the exorcist himself : after this you shall see an infinite com-

pany

pany of archers, with a great multitude of horrible beasts, which will arrange themselves as if they would devour the companions; nevertheless, fear nothing.

Then the exorcist, holding the pentacle in his hand, let him say, Avoid hence these iniquities, by virtue of the banner of God. Then will the spirits be compelled to obey the exorcist, and the company shall see them no more.

Then let the exorcist, stretching out his hand with the pentacle, say, Behold the pentacle of *Solomon*, which I have brought into your presence; behold the person of the exorcist in the middle of the exorcism, who is armed by God, without fear, and well provided, who potently invocateth and calleth you by exorcising; come, therefore, with speed, by the virtue of these names; Aye Saraye, Aye Saraye; defer not to come, by the eternal names of the living and true God, Eloy, Archima, Rabur, and by the pentacle of Solomon here present, which powerfully reigns over you; and by the virtue of the celestial spirits, your lords; and by the person of the exorcist, in the middle of the exorcism : being conjured, make haste and come, and yield obedience to your master, who is called Octinomos. This being performed, immediately there will be hissings in the four parts of the world, and then immediately you shall see great motions; which when you see, say, Why stay you? Wherefore do you delay? What do you? Prepare yourselves to be, obedient to your master in the name of the Lord, Bathat or Vachat rushing upon Abrac, Abeor coming upon Aberer.

Then they will immediately come in their proper forms; and when you see them before the circle, shew them the pentacle covered with fine linen; uncover it, and say, Behold your confusion if you refuse to be obedient; and suddenly they will appear in a peaceable form, and will say, Ask what you will, for we are prepared to fulfil all your commands, for the Lord hath subjected us hereunto.

Then let the exorcist say, Welcome spirits, or most noble princes, because I have called you through Him to whom every knee doth bow, both of things in heaven, and things in earth, and things under the earth ; in

whose

whose hands are all the kingdoms of kings, neither is there any able to contradict his Majesty. Wherefore, I bind you, that you remain affable and visible before this circle, so long and so constant; neither shall you depart without my licence, until you have truly and without any fallacy performed my will, by virtue of his power who hath set the sea her bounds, beyond which it cannot pass, nor go beyond the law of his providence, *viz.* of the Most High God, Lord, and King, who hath created all things. *Amen.*

Then let the exorcist mention what he would have done.

After which say, In the name of the Father, and of the Son, and of the Holy Ghost, go in peace unto your places; peace be between us and you; be ye ready to come when you are called. (For the figures of the circle, pentacle, and other instruments, see the Plate.)

Now, that you may have an idea of the manner of composing the circle, we have given the scheme of one for the first hour of the Lord's day, in spring.

———

Here follow the CONSIDERATIONS *and* CONJURATIONS *for every Day in the Week; and first of*

The CONSIDERATIONS, *&c. of* SUNDAY.

(For the figure of the *seals*, *planets*, *signs*, names of the angels of the several days, and names of the fourth heaven, with the characters and magic book, see the Plate.)

THE angels of the Lord's day—*Michael, Dardiel, Huratapel.*

The angels of the air ruling on the Lord's day, *Varcan*, king ;—his ministers. *Tus, Andas, Cynabal.*

The wind which the angels of the air are said to rule, is the north wind.

The angels of the fourth heaven ruling on the Lord's day, which should be called from the four parts of the world, are,—east, *Samael, Baciel, Abel, Gabriel,*

Gabriel, Vionatraba ;—from the west, *Anael, Pabel, Ustael, Burchat, Suceratos, Capabili* ;—from the north, *Aiel, Ariel, vel Aquiel, Masgabriel, Saphiel, Matuyel,* —at the south, *Haludiel, Machasiel, Charsiel, Uriel, Naromiel.*

The perfume of Sunday is *Red Sanders.*

The CONJURATION *for* SUNDAY.

I CONJURE and confirm upon you, ye strong and holy angels of God, in the name *Adonai, Eye, Eye, Eya,* which is he who was, and is, and is to come, *Eye, Abray ;* and in the name *Saday, Cados, Cados,* sitting on high upon the *cherubim ;* and by the great name of *God* himself, strong and powerful, who is exalted above all the heavens ; *Eye, Saraye,* who created the world, the heavens, the earth, the sea, and all that in them is, in the first day, and sealed them with his holy name Phaa ; and by the name of the angels who rule in the *fourth heaven,* and serve before the most mighty *Salamia,* an angel great and honourable ; and by the name of his star, which is Sol, and by his sign, and by the immense name of the living *God,* and by all the names aforesaid, I conjure thee, Michael, O great angel ! who art chief ruler of this day ; and by the name Adonai, the God of Israel, I conjure thee, O Michael ! that thou labour for me, and fulfil all my petitions according to my will and desire in my cause and business.

The spirits of the air of the Lord's day are under the north wind ; their nature is to procure gold, gems, carbuncles, diamonds, and rubies, and to cause one to obtain favour and benevolence, to dissolve enmities amongst men, to raise to honours, and to take away infirmities. *They appear,* for the most part, in a large, full and great body, sanguine and gross, in a gold colour, with the tincture of blood. Their motion is like the lightning of heaven ; the sign of their becoming visible is that they move the person to sweat that calls them ; but their particular forms are as follows ; *viz.*

A king, having a scepter, riding on a lion.

A king crowned ; a queen with a scepter.

A bird ;

A bird ; a lion ; a cock.

A yellow garment.

A scepter.

CONSIDERATIONS, &c. of MONDAY.

(For the angel of Monday, his sigil, planet, sign of the planet, and name of
the first heaven, see the Plate.)

THE angels of Monday—*Gabriel, Michael, Samael.*

The angels of the air ruling Monday, *Arcan*, king;—his ministers, *Bilet,
Missabu, Abuhaza.* The wind which these are subject to is the *west wind.*

The angels of the first heaven, ruling on Monday, to be called from
the four parts of the world. From the east, *Gabriel, Madiel, Deamiel,
Janak;*—from the west, *Sachiel, Zaniel, Habiel, Bachanæ, Corobael;*—from
the north, *Mael, Uvael, Valnum, Baliel, Balay, Humastraw;*—from the south,
—*Curaniel, Dabriel, Darquiel, Hanun, Vetuel.*

The perfume of Monday—*Aloes.*

The CONJURATION *of* MONDAY.

I CONJURE and confirm upon you, ye strong and good angels, in the
name *Adonai, Adonai, Adonai, Adonai, Eye, Eye, Eye; Cados, Cados, Cados,
Achim, Achim, Ja, Ja,* strong *Ja,* who appeared in mount Sinai with the
glorification of king *Adonai, Sadai,* Zebaoth, Anathay, Ya, Ya, Ya, Maranata,
Abim, Jeia, who created the sea, and all lakes and waters, in the second day,
which are above the heavens and in the earth, and sealed the sea in his high
name, and gave it its bounds beyond which it cannot pass; and by the names
of the angels who rule in the *first legion,* and who serve *Orphaniel,* a great,
precious, and honourable angel, and by the name of his star which is Luna, and
by all the names aforesaid, I conjure thee, *Gabriel,* who art chief ruler of
Monday, the second day, that for me thou labour and fulfil, &c.

The

The spirits of the air of Monday are subject to the west wind, which is the wind of the moon; their nature is to give silver and to convey things from place to place; to make horses swift, and to disclose the secrets of persons both present and future.

Their familiar Forms are as follow:

They appear generally of a great and full stature, soft and phlegmatic, of colour like a black, obscure cloud, having a swoln countenance, with eyes red and full of water, a bald head, and teeth like a wild boar; their motion is like an exceeding great tempest of the sea. For their sign there will appear an exceeding great rain, and their particular shapes are,

A king, like an archer, riding upon a doe.

A little boy.

A woman-hunter with a bow and arrows.

A cow; a little doe; a goose.

A green, or silver-coloured garment.

An arrow; a creature with many feet.

CONSIDERATIONS *of* TUESDAY.

(For the angel of Tuesday, his sigil, planet, sign governing the planet, and name of the fifth heaven, see the Plate.)

THE angels of the air on Tuesday—*Samael, Satael, Amabiel.*

The angels of the air ruling on Tuesday, *Samax,* king; his Ministers, *Carmax, Ismoli, Paffran.*

The wind to which the said angels are subject is the *east wind.*

The angels of the fifth heaven ruling on Tuesday.—At the east, *Friagne, Guel, Damael, Calzas, Arragon;*---the west, *Lama, Astagna, Lobquin, Soneas, Jazel, Isiael, Irel;*---the north, *Rhaumel, Hyniel, Rayel, Seraphiel, Fraciel, Mathiel;*---the south, *Sacriel, Janiel, Galdel, Osael, Vianuel, Zaliel.*

The perfume of Tuesday---*Pepper.*

The

The CONJURATION *of* TUESDAY.

I CONJURE and call upon you, ye strong and good angels, in the names Ya, Ya, Ya; He, He, He; Va, Hy, Hy, Ha, Ha, Ha; Va, Va, Va; An, An, An; Aia, Aia, Aia; El, Ay, Elibra, Elohim, Elohim; and by the names of the high God, who hath made the sea and dry land, and by his word hath made the earth, and produced trees, and hath set his seal upon the planets, with his precious, honoured, revered and holy name; and by the name of the angels governing in the fifth house, who are subservient to the great angel Acimoy, who is strong, powerful, and honoured, and by the name of his star which is called *Mars*, I call upon thee, *Samael*, by the names above mentioned, thou great angel! who presides over the day of *Mars*, and by the name Adonai, the living and true God, that you assist me in accomplishing my labours, *&c. (as in the conjuration of Sunday.)*

The spirits of the air on Tuesday are under the east wind; their nature is to bring or cause war, mortality, death, combustions, and to give two-thousand soldiers at a time; to bring death, infirmity or health.

Familiar Forms of the SPIRITS *of* MARS.

THEY appear in a tall body and choleric, a filthy countenance, of colour brown, swarthy, or red, having horns like harts, and griffins claws, and bellowing like wild bulls. Their motion is like fire burning: their sign thunder and lightning round about the circle.

Their particular shapes are, a king armed, riding on a wolf; a man armed.

A woman with a buckler on her thigh.

A she-goat; a horse; a stag.

A red garment; a piece of wool; a cowslip.

CON-

CONSIDERATIONS *of* WEDNESDAY.

(For the angel of Wednesday his sigil, *&c. &c.* see the Plate.)

THE angels of Wednesday—*Raphael, Meil, Seraphiel.*

The angels of the air ruling on Wednesday, *Mediat*, king; Ministers, *Suquinos, Sallales ;* the said angels of the air are subject to the *south-west wind.*

The angels of the second heaven, governing Wednesday, that are to be called, *&c.* At the east—*Mathlai, Tarmiel, Baraborat*—at the west, *Jeruscue, Merattron ;*—at the north, *Thiel, Rael, Jarihael, Venahel, Velel, Abuiori, Ucirmiel*—at the south, *Milliel, Nelapa, Calvel, vel Laquel.*

The perfume of Wednesday---*Mastic.*

The CONJURATION *of* WEDNESDAY.

I CONJURE and call upon you, ye strong and holy angels, good and powerful, in a strong name of fear and praise, Ja, Adonay, Elohim, Saday, Saday, Saday; Eie, Eie, Eie; Asamie, Asamie; and in the name of Adonay, the God of Israel, who hath made the two great lights, and distinguished day from night for the benefit of his creatures ; and by the names of all the discerning angels, governing openly in the second house before the great angel, *Tetra*, strong and powerful; and by the name of his star which is *Mercury ;* and by the name of his seal, which is that of a powerful and honoured God ; and I call upon thee, Raphael, and by the names above mentioned, thou great angel who presidest over the fourth day : and by the holy name which is written in the front of Aaron, created the most high priest, and by the names of all the angels who are constant in the grace of Christ, and by the name and place of Ammaluim, that you assist me in my labours, *&c. &c.*

The spirits of the air, on Wednesday are subject to the south-west wind ; their nature is to give all sorts of metals, to reveal all earthly things past, present,

BOOK II.   sent,

sent, and to come ; to pacify judges, to give victory in war, to teach experiments and all sciences decayed, and to change bodies mixt of elements, conditionally, out of one thing into another; to give health or infirmities, to raise the poor and cast down the rich, to bind or loose spirits, to open locks or bolts.

Such kinds of spirits have the operations of others, but not in their perfect power, but in virtue or knowledge.

Forms of the Spirits of Mercury.

THE spirits of Mercury appear in a body of a middle stature, cold, liquid and moist, fair and of an affable speech in a human shape and form, like a knight armed, of colour clear and bright. The motion of them is like silver coloured clouds : for their sign they cause horror and fear to him that calls them.

Their particular shapes are, a king riding upon a bear.

A fair youth ; a woman holding a distaff.

A dog, a she-bear, and a magpye.

A garment of various changeable colours.

A rod, a little staff.

Considerations of Thursday.

(For the angel of Thursday, his sigil, &c. see the Plate.)

THE angels of Thursday---*Sachiel, Cassiel, Asasiel.*

The angels of the air of Thursday, *Suth,* king; Ministers, *Maguth, Gutrix.*

The angels of the air are under the south-wind.—(But because there are no angels of the air to be found above the fifth heaven, therefore, on Thursday, say the prayers following in the four parts of the world :)

At the east—*O Deus magne et excelse et honorate, per infinita secula;* or, O great and most high God, honoured be thy name, world without end.

At

At the west—O wise, pure, and just God, of divine clemency, I beseech thee, most holy Father, that this day I may perfectly understand and accomplish my petition, work, and labour; for the honour and glory of thy holy name, who livest and reignest, world without end. *Amen.*

At the north—O God, strong, mighty, and wonderful, from everlasting to everlasting, grant that this day I bring to effect that which I desire, through our blessed Lord. *Amen.*

At the south—O mighty and most merciful God, hear my prayers and grant my petition.

The perfume of Thursday—*Saffron.*

The CONJURATION *of* THURSDAY.

I CONJURE and confirm upon you, ye strong and holy angels, by the names Cados, Cados, Cados, Eschereie, Escherei, Eschereie, Hatim, Ya, strong founder of the worlds; Cantine, Jaym, Janic, Anic, Calbot, Sabbac, Berisay, Alnaym; and by the name Adonai, who created fishes and creeping things in the waters, and birds upon the face of the earth, flying towards heaven, in the fifth day; and by the names of the angels serving in the sixth host before Pastor, a holy angel, and a great and powerful prince and by the name of his star, which is Jupiter, and by the name of his seal, and by the name of Adonai, the great God, Creator of all things, and by the name of all the stars, and by their power and virtue, and by all the names aforesaid, I conjure thee, Sachiel, a great Angel, who art chief ruler of Thursday, that for me thou labour, *&c.*

The spirits of the air of Thursday are subject to the south wind; their nature is to procure the love of women, to cause men to be merry and joyful, to pacify strifes and contentions, to appease enemies, to heal the diseased, and to disease the whole, and procure losses, or restore things lost.

The

The familiar Forms of the SPIRITS *of* JUPITER.

They appear with a body sanguine and choleric, of a middle stature, with a horrible, fearful motion, but with a mild countenance, and a gentle speech, and of the colour of iron : the motion of them is flashings of lightning, and thunder. For their sign there will appear about the circle men who shall seem to be devoured by lions. Their forms are,

A king, with a sword drawn, riding on a stag.

A man, wearing a mitre, with long raiment.

A maid, with a laurel crown, adorned with flowers.

A bull ; a stag ; a peacock.

An azure garment ; a sword ; a box-tree,

CONSIDERATIONS *of* FRIDAY.

(For the seal planet, and sign governing the planet, and name of the third heaven, see the Plate.)

THE angels of Friday—*Anael, Rachiel, Sachiel.*

The angels of the air ruling on Friday, *Sarabotes,* king; Ministers, *Amahiel, Aba, Abalidoth, Blaef.* The wind which the angels of the air are subject to is the west wind.

Angels of the third heaven, which are to be called from the four parts of the world, are

At the east, *Setchiel, Chedusitaniel, Corat, Tamuel, Tenaciel;*—at the west, *Turiel, Coniel, Babiel, Kadie, Maltiel, Huphaltiel;*—at the north, *Peniel, Penael, Penat, Raphael, Ranie, Doremiel;*—at the south, *Porosa, Sachiel, Chermiel, Samael, Santanael, Famiel.*

The perfume of Friday—*Pepperwort.*

The

The CONJURATION *of* FRIDAY.

I CONJURE and confirm upon you, ye strong and holy angels, by the names *On*, *Hey*, *Heya*, *Ja*, *Je*, *Saday*, *Adonai*, and in the name *Sadai*, who created four-footed beasts, and creeping things, and man, in the sixth day, and gave to Adam power over all creatures; wherefore blessed be the name of the Creator in his place; and by the name of the angels serving in the third host, before Dagiel, a great angel, and a strong and powerful prince, and by the name of his star, which is Venus, and by his seal which is holy; and by all the names aforesaid, I conjure upon thee, *Anael*, who art the chief ruler this day, that thou labour for me, *&c.*

The spirits of the air on Friday are subject to the west wind: their nature is to give silver, to incite men, and incline them to luxury, to cause marriages, to allure men to love women, to cause or take away infirmities, and to do all things which have motion.

Their familiar Shapes.

They appear with a fair body, of middle stature, with an amiable and pleasant countenance, of colour white or green, their upper parts golden; the motion of them is like a clear star. For their sign there will appear naked virgins round the circle, which will strive to allure the invocator to dalliance with them: but

Their particular Shapes are,

A king, with a scepter, riding on a camel.

A naked girl; a she-goat.

A camel; a dove.

A white or green garment.

Flowers; the herb savine.

The

The CONSIDERATIONS *of* SATURDAY.

(For seal, *&c. &c.* see the Plate.)

THE angels of Saturday---*Cassiel, Machatan, Uriel.*

The angels of the air ruling this day, *Maymon,* king; Ministers, *Abuma-lith, Assaibi, Balidet.* The wind they are subject to, the *south wind.*

The fumigation of Saturday is *sulphur.*

There are no angels ruling in the air on Saturday above the fifth heaven, therefore in the four corners of the world, in the circle, use those orations which are applied to Thursday.

The CONJURATION *of* SATURDAY.

I CONJURE and confirm upon you, Caphriel, or Cassiel, Machator, and Seraquiel, strong and powerful angels; and by the name Adonai, Adonai, Adonai; Eie, Eie, Eie; Acim, Acim, Acim; Cados, Cados; Ima, Ima, Ima; Salay, Ja, Sar, Lord and Maker of the World, who rested on the seventh day; and by him who of his good pleasure gave the same to be observed by the children of Israel throughout their generations, that they should keep and sanctify the same, to have thereby a good reward in the world to come; and by the names of the *angels* serving in the seventh host, before Booel, a great angel, and powerful prince; and by the name of his star, which is Saturn; and by his holy seal, and by the names before spoken, I conjure upon thee, Caphriel, who art chief ruler of the seventh day, which is the Sabbath, that for me thou labour, *&c. &c.*

The spirits of the air on Saturday are subject to the south-west wind: the nature of them is to sow discords, hatred, evil thoughts and cogitations, to give leave to kill and murder, and to lame or maim every member.

Their

Their familiar Shapes.

THEY generally appear with a tall, lean, slender body, with an angry countenance, having four faces, one on the back of the head, one in the front, and one on each side, nosed or beaked, likewise there appears a face on each knee of a black shining colour; their motion is the moving of the wind, with a kind of earthquake; their sign is white earth, whiter than snow.

Their particular Shapes are,

* A king, bearded, riding on a dragon.
An old man with a beard.
An old woman leaning on a crutch.
A hog; a dragon; an owl.
A black garment; a hook or sickle.
A juniper tree.

Those are the figures that these spirits usually assume, which are generally terrible at the first coming on of the visions, but as they have only a limited power, beyond which they cannot pass, so the invocator need be under no apprehensions of danger, provided he is well fortified with those things we have directed to be used for his defence, and above all, to have a firm and constant faith in the mercy, wisdom, and goodness of God.

---

* Those spirits who appear in a kingly form, have a much higher dignity than them who take an inferior shape; and those who appear in a human shape, exceed in authority and power them that come as animals; and again, these latter surpass in dignity them who appear as trees or instruments, and the like: so that you are to judge of the power, government, and authority of spirits by their assuming a more noble and dignified apparition.

END OF THE THIRD PART, AND OF CABALISTICAL AND CEREMONIAL MAGIC.

The Magic Wand to be used in Invocations by the Chrystal.

Two Holy wax Lights used in the Invocation by the Chrystal.

The true size & form of the Chrystal which must be sett in pure Gold, & the same names & characters as in the model here given.

The magic Circle of a simple construction in which the operator must stand or sit when he uses the Chrystal

Tetragrammaton

Elohim

ADONAI

The Tripod on which the perfumes are put, & may be either held in the hand or sett in the earth.

El. Elohim, Elohe, Zebaoth, Elion, Eserchie, Adonai, Jah, Tetragrammaton, Saday, Jod, Shevi.

מיכאל

Michael

The Lamen, or Holy Table of the Archangel Michael.

Michael

Gabriel

Uriel

Raphael

write or engrave on the other side

Ego Alpha et Omega.

Pub. by .... J. Allen.

MAGIC AND PHILOSOPHY

OF

TRITHEMIUS OF SPANHEIM;

CONTAINING HIS BOOK OF

SECRET THINGS,

AND

DOCTRINE OF SPIRITS:

With many curious and rare Secrets (hitherto not generally known ;)

THE ART OF DRAWING SPIRITS INTO CRYSTALS, &c.

With many other Experiments in the Occult Sciences, never yet published in the English Language.

———

TRANSLATED FROM A VALUABLE LATIN MANUSCRIPT,

By *FRANCIS BARRETT,*

STUDENT OF CHEMISTRY, NATURAL AND OCCULT PHILOSOPHY, THE CABALA, &c.

———

PART IV.

Book II.

MAGIC AND PHILOSOPHY

OF

TRITHEMIUS OF SPANHEIM.

The Translator's LETTER *to a* FRIEND *of his, a young Student in these occult Sciences.*

MY FRIEND,

K NOWING thee to be a curious searcher after those sciences which are out of the common track of study, (I mean the art of foretelling events, magic, telismans, &c.) I am moved spiritually to give thee my thoughts upon them, and by these ideas here written, to open to thine eye (spiritual) as much information as it seems necessary for thee to know, by. which thou mayest be led by the hand into the delectable field of nature; and to give thee such documents as, guided by the supreme wisdom of the Highest, thou mayest refresh thy soul with a delicious draught of knowledge; so that after recreating thy spirit with the use of those good gifts which may please God to bestow on thee, thou mayest be wrapped up into the contemplation of the immense wisdom of that great munificent Being who created thee.

Now, art thou a man, in whose soul the image of Divinity is sealed for eternity, think first what is thy desire in the searching after these mysteries! Is it wealth, honour, fame, power, might, aggrandizement, and the like? Perhaps thy heart says, All! all these I would gladly crave! If so, this is my answer,—seek first to know thyself thoroughly, cleanse thy heart from all wicked, vain, and rapacious desires. Thinkest thou, oh man! to attain power *to gratify thy lusts, to enrich thy coffers, to build houses*, to raise thyself to the pinnacle of human admiration; if these are thy hopes and desires, thou hast reason to lament thy being born: all such desires are immediately from

the

the devil, I mean that Being whose engines (*i. e.* myriads of demons) are conti-nually in the act of placing sensual delights and luxuries before the depraved minds and hearts of man, and whose chief business and property it is to counteract the benevolent actions and inspirations of those blessed spirits who are the instruments of God our Creator.

Fear God and love thy neighbour; use no deceit, swear not, neither lye; let all thy actions be sincere. Here, O man! is the grand seal of all earthly wisdom, the true talisman of human happiness. When thou shalt accom-plish this, behold nothing will be impossible unto thee as far as God permits: then with all speed apply thy mind and heart to attain knowledge and wis-dom; with all humility throw thy dependence on God alone, the author of all things that cannot die.

To know thyself is to know God, for it is a spiritual gift *from God* that enables a man to know himself. This gift but very few possess, as may be daily seen. How many are there tossed about to and fro' upon the perilous sea of contending passions, and who are more light than feathers! how many in this great city who place their chiefest *good* in debauchery and letchery! See their *actions, manners,* and *dispositions*; these poor, unfortunate, miserable wretches, such is their fatal magical infatuation and ignorance, that they think those mad who might even attempt to reason with them on the vanity and misery of their situation. To make myself more intelligible, these are what the world calls men of fashion, a phrase insignificant enough when we consider that the universal fashion of this time is vice, and that so glaring, that it needs no great intellect to discover what is daily open to the view of the observer. But to you, my friend, I have addressed these lines; therefore let it not be supposed that I am reprehending my friend for vices which I cannot suppose him attached to: for I know thou art a young man designed for the receiving of instruction, in much higher and more glorious contemplations than those sons of earth are capable of, therefore I have presented thee with this translation which thou didst desire me to give thee.

But

But beware of flattery, self-love, and covetousness, so wilt thou thrive ; and be diligent in thy occupation, so shall thy body be fed. Idleness is offensive to the Deity, industry shall sweeten thy brown bread, and the fruits of it shall warm thine heart, and inspire thy soul with gratitude to him that blesses thee with *enough :* seek for no more, for it will damn thee ; pray for enough to feed and clothe thy body, but ask no more, lest thou pine away in heart-rending poverty, and spend the remainder of thy days in contumely and beggary. For know a thing most necessary for thee to know, that if by thy study, by thy art, or any other thing, thou couldst *command a million of spirits,* it should not be lawful for thee to wish to gain riches suddenly, for the Wisdom Eternal has put forth the fiat ; and it has been said by him who never spoke in vain, and who cannot lye, *that man shall get bread by the sweat of his brow ;* therefore let us not have in view the enriching of ourselves in worldly goods, by supernatural means, or by a greedy desiring of what we ought to look upon with eyes of contempt, draw upon us the wrath of God. Rather let us cheerfully rely on, and follow in very deed, spirit and truth, these words of the apostle, "Seek ye first the kingdom of God, and all these things shall be added unto you ;" fear not but that God shall make thy household as a flourishing tree, and thy wife shall be as a fruitful vine. Farewell, remember my poor counsel, and be happy. From thy true friend,   F. B.

N. B. To enable thee the better to comprehend this Book, I have drawn out the various figures, of which mention is made in this work, that thou mayest see the very exact method of working ; likewise the images of seals, spirits, and various other rare, and curious instruments, which are necessary for thee to know and see with the eye ; therefore in the construction of them thou canst not be liable to error.

Fig. 1. The form of the crystal for invocating spirits, with the plate of pure gold in which the crystal must be fastened, with the divine characters around.

Fig. 2.

Fig 2.   A magical circle (C D E F), of a simple construction, for the operator to stand or sit in when he calleth the spirits.

Fig. 3.   The crystal (A), two silver or other candlesticks (G G,) with the wax tapers burning, and tripod or vessel for the oderiferous suffumigation.

Fig 4.   A wand of black ebony with golden characters.   The characters are explained.

A C A U T I O N *to the inexperienced in this* A R T, *and a Word of Advice to those who would be Adepts.*

BROTHER,

IT is necessary for me to inform thee, that whatever thy desires are in the pursuit of this art, which we call Magic, so wilt thy connexion and answer be. If in the pursuit of revenge, it is but proper thou shouldest know that thou wilt, in any of these experiments here laid down, draw to thyself a revengeful demon, or an infernal furious spirit, serving in the principle of the wrath of God ; if worldly riches and aggrandizement, then shalt thou have an earthial or fiery spirit, which will delude thee with the riches of the central world ; if fame, or the blaze of glory, then the *spirits of pride* will be allotted thee, who will gratify thy inordinate desire of vain glory ; for all these offices are there spirits allotted and will be eager to mix with thy spirit : it will attract thee to his own nature, and serve all thy purposes according to the extent of God's permission ; and as thy desires are and from what principle they proceed, so shalt thou be answered : but if thou desirest to know nothing but for the honour and glory of God, and the help of thy neighbour, and, in great humility, fill thy heart with the love of God, thou shalt then have a pure spirit which

will

will grant (by the Lord's permission) they desires.   Therefore seek for that which is good; avoid all evil either in thought, word, or action; pray to God to fill thee with wisdom, and then thou shalt reap an abundant harvest. There are two ways magically set before thee; chuse which thou wilt, thou shalt be sure of thy reward.   Farewel.

London, 1800.   F. B.

Of the making of the CRYSTAL *and the Form of Preparation for a*
VISION.

PROCURE of a lapidary good clear pellucid crystal, of the bigness of a small orange, *i. e.* about one inch and a half in diameter; let it be glo-bular or round each way alike; then, when you have got this crystal, fair and clear, without any clouds or specks, get a small plate of pure gold to encom-pass the crystal round one half; let this be fitted on an ivory or ebony pedestal, as you may see more fully described in the drawing, (see the Plate, fig. 1.) Let there be engraved a circle (A) round the crystal with these characters around inside the circle next the crystal ; afterwards the name " *Tetragrammaton* ".   On the other side of the plate let there be engra-ven " *Michael, Gabriel, Uriel, Raphael;* " which are the four principal angels ruling over the *Sun, Moon, Venus* and *Mercury;* but on the table on which the crystal stands the following names, characters, &c. must be drawn in order.

First, The names of the seven planets and angels ruling them, with their seals or characters.   The names of the four kings of the four corners of the earth.   Let them be all written within a double circle, with a triangle on a table; on which place the crystal on its pedestal: this being done,

thy

thy table is complete (as in the Fig. D,) and fit for the calling of the spirits; after which thou shalt proceed to experiment, thus :

In what time thou wouldest deal with the spirits by the *table* and *crystal*, thou must observe the planetary hour; and whatever planet rules in that hour, the angel governing the planet thou shalt call in the manner following; but first, say this short prayer :

" Oh, God! who art the author of all good things, strengthen, I beseech thee, thy poor servant, that he may stand fast, without fear, through this dealing and work; enlighten, I beseech thee, oh Lord! the dark understanding of thy creature, so that his spiritual eye may be opened to see and know thy angelic spirits descending here in this crystal : (*Then lay thy hand on the crystal saying,*) and thou, oh inanimate creature of God, be sanctified and consecrated, and blessed to this purpose, that no evil phantasy may appear in thee ; or, if they do gain ingress into this creature, they may be constrained to speak intelligibly, and truly, and without the least ambiguity, for Christ's sake. *Amen.* And forasmuch as thy servant here standing before thee, oh, Lord! desires neither evil treasures, nor injury to his neighbour, nor hurt to any living creature, grant him the power of descrying those celestial spirits or intelligences, that may appear in this crystal, and whatever good gifts (whether the power of healing infirmities, or of imbibing wisdom, or discovering any evil likely to afflict any person or family, or any other good gift thou mayest be pleased to bestow on me, enable me, by thy wisdom and mercy, to use whatever I may receive to the honour of thy holy name. Grant this for thy son Christ's sake. *Amen.*"

Then taking your ring and pentacle, put the ring on the little finger of your right hand; hang the pentacle round thy neck ; (*Note*, the pentacle may be either wrote on clean virgin parchment, or engraven on a square plate of silver and suspended from thy neck to the breast), then take your black ebony wand, with the gilt characters on it and trace the circle, (Fig. 7. C D E F,) saying, " In the name of the blessed Trinity, I consecrate this piece of ground for our defence ; so that no evil spirit may have power to break these bounds prescribed here, through Jesus Christ our Lord." *Amen.*

Then

Then place the vessel for the perfumes between thy circle and the holy table on which the crystal stands, and, having fire therein, cast in thy perfumes, saying,

"I conjure thee, oh thou creature of fire! by him who created all things both in heaven and earth, and in the sea, and in every other place whatever, that forthwith thou cast away every phantasm from thee, that no hurt whatsoever shall be done in any thing. Bless, oh Lord, this creature of fire, and sanctify it that it may be blessed, and that they may fill up the power and virtue of their odours; so neither the enemy, nor any false imagination, may enter into them; through our Lord Jesus Christ. *Amen.*"

Now, this being done in the order prescribed, take out thy little book, which must be made about seven inches long, of pure white virgin vellum or paper, likewise pen and ink must be ready to write down the *name*, *character*, and *office*, likewise the seal or image of whatever spirit may appear (for this I must tell you that it does not happen that the same spirit you call will always appear, for you must try the spirit to know whether he be a pure or impure being, and this thou shalt easily know by a firm and undoubted faith in God.)

Now the most pure and simple way of calling the spirits or spirit is by a short oration to the spirit himself, which is more effectual and easy to perform than composing a table of letters; for all celestial operations, the more pure and unmixed they are, the more they are agreable to the celestial spirits: therefore, after the circle is drawn, the book, perfumes, rod, *&c.* in readiness, proceed as follows:

(After noticing the exact hour of the day, and what angel rules that hour, thou shalt say,)

"In the name of the blessed and holy Trinity, I do desire thee, thou strong and mighty angel *, Michæl, that if it be the divine will of him who is called Tetragrammaton, &c. the Holy God, the Father, that thou take upon thee some shape as best becometh thy celestial nature, and appear to us visibly here in this crystal, and answer our demands in as far as we shall not transgress the

---

* Or any other angel or spirit.

bounds

bounds of the divine mercy and goodness, by requesting unlawful knowledge; but that thou wilt graciously shew us what things are most profitable for us to know and do, to the glory and honour of his divine Majesty, who liveth and reigneth, world without end. *Amen.*

" Lord, thy will be done on earth, as it is in heaven;—make clean our hearts within us, and take not thy Holy Spirit from us.

" O Lord, by thy name, we have called him, suffer him to administer unto us. And that all things may work together for thy honour and glory, to whom with thee, the Son, and blessed Spirit, be ascribed all might, majesty and dominion. *Amen.*"

Note, In these dealings, two should always be present; for often a spirit is manifest to one in the crystal when the other cannot perceive him; therefore if any spirit appear, as there most likely will, to one or both, say,

" Oh, Lord! we return thee our hearty and sincere thanks for the hearing of our prayer, and we thank thee for having permitted thy spirit to appear unto us which we, by thy mercy, will interrogate to our further instruction, through Christ. *Amen.*"

Interrog. 1. In the name of the holy and undefiled Spirit, the Father, the begotten Son, and Holy Ghost, proceeding from both, what is thy true name?

If the spirit answers, *Michael,* then proceed.

Quest. 2. What is thy office? 3. What is thy true sign or character? 4. When are the times most agreeable to thy nature to hold conference with us?

Wilt thou swear by the blood and righteousness of our Lord Jesus Christ, that thou art truly Michael?

(Here let him swear, then write down his seal or character in thy book, and against it, his office and times to be called, through God's name; also write down any thing he may teach thee, or any responses he may make to thy questions or interrogations, concerning life or death, arts or sciences, or any other thing ;) and then shalt thou say,

" Thou

" Thou great and mighty spirit, inasmuch as thou camest in peace and in the name of the ever blessed and righteous Trinity, so in this name thou mayest depart, and return to us when we call thee in his name to whom every knee doth bow down.   Fare thee well, Michael; peace be between us, through our blessed Lord Jesus Christ. *Amen."*

Then will the spirit depart; then say, " To God the Father, eternal Spirit, fountain of Light, the Son, and Holy Ghost, be all honour and glory, world without end. *Amen."*

I shall here set down the Table of the names of Spirits and Planets governing the Hours; so thou shalt easily know by inspection, what Spirit and Planet governs every Hour of the Day and Night in the Week.

Hours Day.	Angels and Planets ruling SUNDAY.	Angels and Planets ruling MONDAY.	Angels and Planets ruling TUESDAY.	Angels and Planets ruling WEDNESDAY.	Angels and Planets ruling THURSDAY.	Angels and Planets ruling FRIDAY.	Angels and Planets ruling SATURDAY.
	Day.	*Day.*	*Day.*	*Day.*	*Day.*	*Day.*	*Day.*
1	⊙ Michael	☽ Gabriel	♂ Samael	☿ Raphael	♃ Sachiel	♀ Anael	♄ Cassiel
2	♀ Anael	♄ Cassiel	⊙ Michael	☽ Gabriel	♂ Samael	☿ Raphael	♃ Sachiel
3	☿ Raphael	♃ Sachiel	♀ Anael	♄ Cassiel	⊙ Michael	☽ Gabriel	♂ Samael
4	☽ Gabriel	♂ Samael	☿ Raphael	♃ Sachiel	♀ Anael	♄ Cassiel	⊙ Michael
5	♄ Cassiel	⊙ Michael	☽ Gabriel	♂ Samael	☿ Raphael	♃ Sachiel	♀ Anael
6	♃ Sachiel	♀ Anael	♄ Cassiel	⊙ Michael	☽ Gabriel	♂ Samael	☿ Raphael
7	♂ Samael	☿ Raphael	♃ Sachiel	♀ Anael	♄ Cassiel	⊙ Michael	☽ Gabriel
8	⊙ Michael	☽ Gabriel	♂ Samael	☿ Raphael	♃ Sachiel	♀ Anael	♄ Cassiel
9	♀ Anael	♄ Cassiel	⊙ Michael	☽ Gabriel	♂ Samael	☿ Raphael	♃ Sachiel
10	☿ Raphael	♃ Sachiel	♀ Anael	♄ Cassiel	⊙ Michael	☽ Gabriel	♂ Samael
11	☽ Gabriel	♂ Samael	☿ Raphael	♃ Sachael	♀ Anael	♄ Cassiel	⊙ Michael
12	♄ Cassiel	⊙ Michael	☽ Gabriel	♂ Samael	☿ Raphael	♃ Sachiel	♀ Anael
Hours Night	*Night.*	*Night.*	*Night.*	*Night.*	*Night.*	*Night.*	*Night.*
1	♃ Sachael	♀ Anael	♄ Cassiel	⊙ Michael	☽ Gabriel	♂ Samael	☿ Raphael
2	♂ Samiel	☿ Raphael	♃ Sachiel	♀ Anael	♄ Cassiel	⊙ Michael	☽ Gabriel
3	⊙ Michael	☽ Gabriel	♂ Samael	☿ Raphael	♃ Sachiel	♀ Anael	♄ Cassiel
4	♀ Anael	♄ Cassiel	⊙ Michael	☽ Gabriel	♂ Samael	☿ Raphael	♃ Sachiel
5	☿ Raphael	♃ Sachiel	♀ Anael	♄ Cassiel	⊙ Michael	☽ Gabriel	♂ Samael
6	☽ Gabriel	♂ Samael	☿ Raphael	♃ Sachiel	♀ Anael	♄ Cassiel	⊙ Michael
7	♄ Cassiel	⊙ Michael	☽ Gabriel	♂ Samael	☿ Raphael	♃ Sachiel	♀ Anael
8	♃ Sachiel	♀ Anael	♄ Cassiel	⊙ Michael	☽ Gabriel	♂ Samael	☿ Raphael
9	♂ Samael	☿ Raphael	♃ Sachiel	♀ Anael	♄ Cassiel	⊙ Michael	☽ Gabriel
10	⊙ Michael	☽ Gabriel	♂ Samael	☿ Raphael	♃ Sachiel	♀ Anael	♄ Cassiel
11	♀ Anael	♄ Cassiel	⊙ Michael	☽ Gabriel	♂ Samael	☿ Raphael	♃ Sachiel
12	☿ Raphael	♃ Sachiel	♀ Anael	♄ Cassiel	⊙ Michael	☽ Gabriel	♂ Samael

Note,

Note, The day is divided into twelve equal parts, called Planetary Hours, reckoning from sun-rise to sun-set, and, again, from the setting to the rising; and to find the planetary hour, you need but to divide the natural hours by twelve, and the quotient gives the length of the planetary hours and odd minuets, which shews you how long a spirit bears rule in that day; as Michael governs the first and the eighth hour on Sunday, as does the ☉. After you have the length of the first hour, you have only to look in the Table, as if it be the fourth hour, on Sunday, you see in the Table that the ☽ and Gabriel rules; and so for the rest it being so plain and easy you cannot err.

THE CONCLUSION OF THE MAGUS.

ADVERTISEMENT.

THE Author of this Work respectfully informs those who are curious in the studies of Art and Nature, especially of Natural and Occult Philosophy, Chemistry, Astrology, &c. &c. that, having been indefatigable in his researches into those sublime Sciences, of which he has treated at large in this Book, that he gives private instructions and lectures upon any of the above-mentioned Sciences; in the course of which he will discover many curious and rare experiments. Those who become Students will be initiated into the choicest operations of Natural Philosophy, Natural Magic, the Cabala, Chemistry, the Talismanic Art, Hermetic Philosophy, Astrology, Physiognomy, &c. &c. Likewise they will acquire the knowledge of the Rites, Mysteries, Ceremonies, and Principles of the ancient Philosophers, Magi, Cabalists, Adepts, &c.—The purpose of this School (which will consist of no greater number than Twelve Students) being to investigate the hidden treasures of Nature; to bring the Mind to a contemplation of the Eternal Wisdom; to promote the discovery of whatever may conduce to the perfection of Man; the alleviating the miseries and calamities of this life, both in respect of ourselves and others; the study of morality and religion here, in order to secure to ourselves felicity hereafter; and, finally, the promulgation of whatever may conduce to the general happiness and welfare of mankind.——Those who feel themselves thoroughly disposed to enter upon such a course of studies, as is above recited, with the same principles of philanthropy with which the Author invites the lovers of philosophy and wisdom, to incorporate themselves in so select, permanent, and desirable a society, may speak with the Author upon the subject, at any time between the hours of Eleven and Two o'clock, at 99 Norton Street, Mary-le-Bonne.

Letters (post paid) upon any subject treated of in this Book, will be duly answered, with the necessary information.

BIOGRAPHIA ANTIQUA;

OR,

AN ACCOUNT OF THE LIVES AND WRITINGS

OF THE ANCIENT AND MODERN

MAGI, CABALISTS, AND PHILOSOPHERS,

DISCOVERING THE

PRINCIPLES AND TENETS OF THE FIRST FOUNDERS

OF THE

MAGICAL AND OCCULT SCIENCES:

WHEREIN THE MYSTERIES OF THE PYTHAGORIANS, GYMNOSOPHISTS, EGYPTIANS, BRAGMANNI,
BABYLONIANS, PERSIANS, ETHIOPIANS, CHALDEANS, &c. ARE DISCOVERED:

Including a particular and interesting Account of

ZOROASTER, THE SON OF OROMASIUS,

THE FIRST INSTITUTOR OF PHILOSOPHY BY FIRE, AND MAGIC;

LIKEWISE OF

HERMES TRISMEGISTUS, THE EGYPTIAN,

And other Philosophers, famous for their Learning, Piety, and Wisdom.

TO WHICH IS ADDED

A SHORT ESSAY,

Proving that the First Christians were Magicians, who foretold, acknowledged, and worshipped

THE SAVIOUR OF THE WORLD,

AND

FIRST FOUNDER OF THE CHRISTIAN RELIGION.

BIOGRAPHIA ANTIQUA.

ZOROASTER, THE SON OF OROMASIUS,

FIRST INSTITUTOR OF PHILOSOPHY BY FIRE, AND MAGIC.

ZOROASTER, the son of Oromasius, flourished in the reign of Darius, the successor of Cambyses. * All authors are full of variations in their accounts of this famous person, some making him of a much later date than others; however, we shall give what we have collected from those who appear most authentic, not omitting the traditional history extant amongst the Magi, with which our readers may compare the several stories of biographers, and accept that account which shall seem to them the most rational. Zoroaster, king of the Bactrians, was vanquished by Ninus, and passed for the inventor of magic †. Eusebius places this victory of Ninus in the seventh year of Abraham:

---

* The Author regrets, that, notwithstanding his laborious researches to obtain an authentic and satisfactory account of Zoroaster to present to his readers; that a few generals, and not particulars, can only be given: indeed, the most serious and respectable historians differ so widely in their accounts of him that nothing certain can from thence be deduced: however, we have above recited several authorities to which we have annexed various notes and commentations.

† *Passed for the inventor of magic.*—It is to be noted that he was the inventor of it, and the first of the magi. Justin informs us that this victory was the last of Ninus; that Zoroaster philosophized most judiciously upon the nature and influences of the stars, and on the principles of the universe. Thomas Stanleius, Hist. of Philos. Orientalis, lib. I. cap. iii. informs us that Zoroaster, according to Eusebius, was cotemporary with Semiramis; but it is certain, according to Eusebius, that he was vanquished by king Ninus. Arnobius, lib. I. pa. m. 5. says, "Anciently the Assyrians and Bactrians, "the former under the conduct of Ninus, and the latter under Zoroaster, fought against each " other, not only with men and weapons, but also by the help of magic, and the secret discipline of the Chaldeans." Hermippus, who has wrote cautiously on every thing relative to magic, and explained twenty thousand verses composed by Zoroaster, relates, that one Azonaces initiated

him

Abraham; now several authors make Zoroaster appear much earlier. It has been reported that Zoroaster laughed on the same day he was born, and that he

him into this art, and that he lived 5,000 years before the Trojan war. St. Augustin and Orosius have followed the tradition mentioned by Justin. Apuleius, in his Catalogue of all the most famous Magicians of Antiquity, with great justice places Zoroaster in the first rank, and proves him the most ancient of all : " *Magicarum artium fuisse perhibeter inventor Zoroastres.*" Augustin. de Civitat. Dei, lib. 21. cap. xiv. Eudoxus, who esteemed the art of magic to be accounted the noblest and most useful of all worldly knowledge, relates that Zoroaster lived six thousand years before the death of Plato. Note, that the same thing is affirmed by Aristotle. Agathias, who lived in the reign of Justinian, informs us, that, according to the Persians of that time, Zoroaster and Hystaspes were cotemporary; but they do not say whether this Hystaspes was father to Darius or any other. Sir John Marsham positively decides that he was the father of Darius ; and grounds his opinion on this, that one of the elogies engraven on the tomb makes him the instructor of the Magi ; and that the same historian who makes Hystaspes excel in magic, calls him the father of Darius. Ammianus Marcellinus, lib. 23, pag. m. 324. says, " After the time of Zoroaster, reigned Hystaspes, a very prudent king, and the " father of Darius. This prince, having boldly penetrated into the remotest parts of the Upper India, " came at length to a solitary forest, where there dwelt, in awful and silent tranquility, the Brachmans. " In this peaceful solitude they instructed him in the knowledge of the earth's motion, likewise of the " stars ; and from them he learned the pure and sacred rites of religion. Part of this knowledge he " communicated to the Magi, which, together with the art of predicting future events, they delivered " down to posterity, each in his own family. The great number of men who have descended from " these families, ever since that age down to the present, have all been set apart for cultivating the " knowledge of the Gods." But Ammianus Mercellinus was wrong in saying, that this father of Da- rius was a king ; and no doubt he committed this blunder by having read in general that one king Hystaspes was a great magician, and thought there was no other Hystaspes than the father of Darius. But it is beyond dispute, that one Hystaspes, older than the foundation of Rome, and a great prophet, is mentioned by authors. " Hystaspes also, the most ancient king of the Medes, and from whom the river " Hystaspes derives its name, is the most admirable of them all ; for under the interpretation of the pro- " phecy of a boy, he informed posterity that the Roman empire, nay, even the Roman name, should be " utterly destroyed ; and this he predicted a long time before the establishment of that colony of Trojans," Lactant. lib. VII. cap. xv. pag. m. 492. Justin Martyr informs us, that he predicted the general con- flagration of all perishable things, Justin Apolog. ii. pag. 66. It is affirmed that Pythagoras was Zo- roaster's disciple, under the reign of Cambyses, the son of Cyrus : the words of Apuleius inform us of the fact. Some say that Pythagoras having been made a slave in Egypt, was transported into Persia ; others will have transported him into Babylon, and there instructed by Zoroaster the Babylonian, whom they distinguish from the Persian. We find no less than five Zoroasters mentioned in history : to these five may be added a sixth, mentioned by Apuleius. This Zoroaster lived in Babylon at the time Py- thagoras was brought thither by Cambyses. The same writer calls him " the chief interpreter of all divine mysteries," and says that Pythagoras was chiefly instructed by him. He appears to be the same with he was the only one to whom this happened, and that the palpitation of his brain was so strong as to repulse the hand, it being laid to his head, which they say was a presage of his future knowledge and wisdom. It is added, that he passed twenty years in the deserts, and there eat nothing but a sort of cheese which was never the worse for age; that the love of wisdom and justice obliged him to retire from the world to a mountain, where he lived in solitude; but when he come down from thence there fell a celestial fire upon it, which perpetually burned; that the king of Persia, accompanied with the greatest lords of his court, approached it for the purpose of putting up prayers to God; that Zoroaster came out from these flames unhurt; that he comforted and encouraged the Persians, and offered sacrifices for them to God; that, afterwards, he did not live indifferently with all sorts of men, but only those who were born for truth, and who were capable of the true knowledge of God, which kind of people are called among the Persians, Magi; that he desired his end might be this, viz. to be struck with thunder, and consumed by celestial fire; and that he requested the Persians to collect his ashes, after he was consumed in this manner, and to preserve and venerate them as a pledge of the preservation of their monarchy; that they for a length of time paid great veneration to the relics of Zoroaster, but at length, neglecting them, their monarchy fell to ruin and decay *. The Chronicle of Alexandria adds, that having held this discourse

with Zabratus, by whom Diogenes affirms Pythagoras was purged from all his former filth, and instructed in what is essentially necessary for good men to know, viz. God, nature, and philosophy: he is also the same with Nazaratus, the Assyrian, whom Alexander, in his book of the Pythagorical symbols, affirms to have taught Pythagoras. The same person Suidas calls *Zares*, Cyrillus, *Zaranes*, and Plutarch, *Zarates*.

* According to the tradition of the Magi, we shall explain this fabulous and figurative description of Zoroaster's end. The truth is, he enjoined the Persians rigidly to persevere in the laws he had framed, and the doctrine he had been at the labour to establish, which was, to live in the practice of moral virtue, to avoid all species of luxury, to promote the liberal sciences, to govern all their actions with prudence and integrity, and to meet misfortune with resolution, and to encounter it with philosophy, and to endure the unavoidable calamities of life with fortitude: these, his disciplines, he left as a precious relic among them; which while they strictly adhered to, they need be under no apprehension of tyranny and oppression

discourse with them he invoked Orion, and was consumed by celestial fire. Many will have it that Ham was the Zoroaster of the eastern nations, and the inventor of magic. Mr. Bochart refutes this falsity. Cedrenus observes that Zoroaster, who became so famous for wisdom among the Persians, was descended from Belus : this imports that he was descended from Nimrod. Some authors have taken him for Nimrod ; others for Assur or Japhet. The ancient Persians believe that Zoroaster was before Moses *. Some maintain he was the prophet Ezekiel, and it cannot be denied that they ground their opinions on the agreement of numerous particulars which belong to the one, and are related of the other. George Hornius foolishly imagines that he was the false prophet Balaam. Huetius shews that he was the Moses of the Jews, and mentions an infinite number of particulars in which the accounts we have of Moses agree with the stories related of Zoroaster.—How near all or any of these come to the probability of truth will appear in the sequel, where we have given the most probable and rational account of him, as far as we have been able to trace, from the tradition of the Magi, which we prefer before the confused and partial accounts vulgarly extant. They who believe that Zoroaster pro-

oppression :—these they collected, and for some space of time religiously followed the precepts of this great philosopher : at length, human frailty and vice, corrupting their manners, caused them to relax from their duties, upon which their empire fell into ruin and decay. The idolatry falsely imputed to this wise man, *viz.* his instituting the worshipping of fire, is thus to be interpreted.—Under the celestial symbol of fire was meant truth :—truth he ascribed purely as the great and wonderful attribute of the Godhead, which he acknowledged and worshipped, to wit, one only God, the eternal fire of wisdom and everlasting truth, justice, and mercy !—His magic was the study of the religious worship of that Eternal Being. After Zoroaster, there were four persons chosen to educate the successor of the king of Persia. They chose the wisest, the most just, the most temperate, and the bravest man that could be found. The wisest man (*viz.* one of the Magi), instructed him in Zoroaster's magic, the just in government, the brave in war, and the temperate in social virtue and temperance. Now observe, that Zoroaster is called the son of Oromasius, and that Oromasius is the name given by Zoroaster and his disciples to the good God, and this title was really bestowed upon him by the Persians ; therefore, according to Plato, this Persian Magus, on account of his uncommon learning, religion, and wisdom, was, in an allegorical or figurative manner, called the son of God, or the son of wisdom, truth, &c.

* Some Magi affirm that he is the same with Abraham, and frequently call him Ibrahim Zerdascht, which is, Abraham the friend of fire.

fessed

fessed and taught a diabolical magic * are certainly in the wrong; the magic he taught (of which we shall speak more anon) was only the study of the divine nature, and of religious worship. Some have presumed that Zoroaster was the promulgator of a doctrine of two principles †, or two co-eternal causes, one of good

* The preceding note fully explains those erroneous relations of the wisdom of the Magi. Those who desire to see a great many passages which testify that the magic of the Persians, instituted by Zoroaster, was the study of religion, virtue, and wisdom, let them refer to *Brissonius de Regno Persarum*, lib. ii. p. 178, & seq. edit. Commel. 1595; likewise Jul. Cæsar, Bullengerus Eclog. ad Arnobium, p. 346, & seq. Nor are we ignorant that Gabriel Naude hath most learnedly and solidly justified our Zoroaster against the ignorant imputations of necromancy, black art, &c.

† It has been much contended by philosophers whether Zoroaster was the first suggester of this doctrine of the two principles: the one called by the Magi, Oromases the *good*, and Arimanius the *evil* principle. It is certain Zoroaster asserted the one, *viz.* that of the good, or an essential uncreated self-existent principle, the cause of all good, called by him Oromasus, meaning a good God, &c. In respect of the other principle, Arimanius, we must, before we decide either for or against Zoroaster, consider the nature of the thing in its most impartial sense.

Those who ever read Mr. Bernard's Journal (*Nouvelles de la Republique des Lettres, Feb.* 1701, *and March* 1701, *Art. iii. l. i.*) needs not be informed that the Historia Religionis veterum Persarum, published by Dr. Hyde (professor of the oriental languages in the university of Oxford) at Oxford, in the year 1700, 4to, is one of the most excellent pieces that could possibly be written on such a subject. The idea which the learned journalist hath given of this performance is sufficient to convince us that it contains a very curious erudition, and profound discussions, which discover many rare and uncommon particulars of a country which we scarce knew any thing of before. But to come to the point: Dr. Hyde affirms, that the ancient Persians acknowledge no more than one uncreated principle, which was the good principle, or, in one word, God: and that they looked upon the evil principle as a created being. One of the names, or attributes, which they gave to God, was Hormizda; and they called the evil principle, Ahariman; and this is the original of the two Greek words, Ωρομάσδες and Απειμανιος; one of which was the name of the good, and the other of the evil, principle, as we have seen above, in a passage of Plutarch. The Persians affirmed that Abraham was the first founder of their religion. Zoroaster afterwards made some alterations in it; but it is said he made no manner of change with relation to the doctrine of one sole uncreated principle, but that the only innovation in this particular was the giving the name of Light to the good principle, and that of Darkness to the evil one.

From a misconstruction put upon the doctrine of the Magi, some considerable misreports of their tenets have been propagated: I think none more curious than the following—" That a war arose betwixt the army of light and that of darkness, which at last ended in an accommodation, of which the angels were mediators, and the conditions were that the inferior world should be wholly left to the government of Arimanius for the space of 7000 years, after which it should be restored to light. Before the peace, Arimanius had exterminated all the inhabitants of the world. Light had called men to its assistance while they

good, the other of evil things.   Of this doctrine Plutarch takes notice : he says,
" that Zoroaster the magician, who is said to have lived five thousand years
" before the Trojan war, called the good God, Oromazes, and the evil, Arima-
" nius, &c. &c."   See *Plut. de Iside & Osiride, page* 369.

Dr. Hyde, in his excellent treatise on the religion of the ancient Persians,
cites some authors who clear him on this head.   We shall examine whether
they deserve credit.   It is affirmed that he was no idolater, either with respect
to the worship of fire, or that of Mithra *   What appears least uncertain,
amongst

---

they were yet but spirits ; which it did, either to draw them out of Arimanius' territories, or in order to
give them bodies to engage against this enemy.   They accepted the bodies and the fight, on condition
they should be assisted by the light, and should at last overcome Arimanius.   The resurrection shall come
when he shall be vanquished.   This they conclude was the cause of the mixture, and shall be the cause
of the deliverance.   The Greeks were not ignorant that Zoroaster taught a future resurrection.

* The ancient Persian Magi never did divine honours to the sun or any of the stars.   They maintain
they do not adore the sun, but direct themselves towards it when they pray to God.   It has been found
amongst Zoroaster's secret precepts, that we ought to salute the sun, but not that we should adore him
with religious worship.   He proves that their ceremonies might very justly pass for civil honours, and to
this purpose he makes some exceeding curious observations.   He applies to the fire what he says of the
sun.   The bowings and prostrations of the Persians before the holy fire were not a religious observation,
but only a civil one.   The same thing must be attributed to their reported worship of fire, which, as I
have said above, they kept in their *Pyrea* in imitation of the Jews.   For though they paid a certain reverence to the fire, and that by prostration, yet this was not a religious, only a civil, worship ; as it is from
the force of custom that the eastern people prostrate themselves before any great man ; (so they might
with as much propriety be said to adore or worship him.)   Believe me we ought to be the last to censure
the eastern people with such gross idolatry as has been represented.   The Persians, who have always
been devoted to the highest study of wisdom, performed their duties in life for the honour of their God ;
and, although unenlightened and Barbarians, lived as men, and not as irrational creatures : whereas we,
who know our duty so well, yet practise it so ill : for I may truly say, that notwithstanding the great
benefits we derive from the divine precepts of Christianity, yet I believe it will be found an incontro-
vertible fact that man to man is a serpent, a few individuals excepted.   But to return to our subject :
It was the ancient custom to fall prostrate to angels, as being the messengers and representatives of God.
Besides, there are many examples of this kind of worship, not only in the Old, but New Testament, where
the women who had been converted to the true faith, upon seeing the angels at the sepulchre of Christ,
fell with their faces to the ground and worshipped.   Yet they well knew that it was not God they saw,
but his angels, as appears from their own confession—" we have seen a vision of angels."   Therefore
they are wrongfully called *Idolaters* and worshippers of fire, for Zoroaster was the instrument of their
continuation in the true faith.   He was a man who had the knowledge of the true God, whom he
peculiarly

amongst so many things that are related of him is, that he was the introducer of a new religion into Persia, and that he did it about the reign of Darius the successor of Cambyses : he is still in great veneration among those Persians who are not of the Mahometan religion, but still retain the ancient worship of their country. They call him Zardhust, and several believe that he came from China, and relate many miraculous things on that head. Several authors affirm, that all the books published hitherto under Zoroaster's name, some of which are yet extant, are supposititious. Dr. Hyde dissents from this opinion. *Suidas* affirms, that there were extant four books of Zoroaster : the first, " Of Nature," a book of the Virtues of precious Stones, called de Gemmis ; and five books of Astrology and Astronomy, " Prædictiones ex Inspectione Stellarum." It is very likely that what Pliny relates, as quoted from Zoroaster, was taken from those books, *Plin.* lib. xviii, cap. 24. Eusebius recites a passage which contains a magnificent description of God, and gives it as the very words of Zoroaster in his sacred commentary on the Persian rites. Clemens Alexandrinus says, that the followers of Prodicus boasted of having the secrets or secret books of Zoroaster. But most likely he meant that they boasted of having the secret books of Pythagoras. They were printed, together with the verses of the Sybils at Amsterdam, in the year 1689, according to Opsopæus's edition, Oracula Magica Zoroastris, cum Scholiis Plethonis & Pselli.

peculiarly worshipped in a natural cave, in which he placed several symbols representing the world ; Mithra, representing the sun, filled the master's place. But it was not Mithra, but the true God, that he adored : and, lastly, as he was a true philosopher, a profound alchemist, greatly informed in all the arts of the mathematics, strict and austere in his religion, he struck the Persians with an admiration of him, and by these means made them attentive to his doctrine. The sum of all is, that he lived in a cave, dedicated to the service of God, and the study of all natural and supernatural knowledge ; that he was divinely illuminated, knew the courses of the stars, and the occult and common properties of all compounded and earthly things ; that by fire and Geometry (*i. e.* by Chemistry and the Mathematics) he investigated, proved, and demonstrated, the truth and purity, or else the fugacity and vileness, of all things knowable in this mortal state of humanity. So that the fame, sagacity, wisdom, and virtue of Zoroaster induced some certain men wickedly and fraudulently to impose upon the unwary some false magical oracles, and diabolical inventions, written in Greek and Latin, &c. as the genuine works of the divine and illustrious Zoroaster.

HERMES,

HERMES, SURNAMED TRISMEGISTUS,

OR THE

THRICE GREATEST INTELLIGENCER.

————◆————

HERMES Trismegistus, (who was the author of the divine Pymander and some other books,) lived some time before Moses. He received the name of Trismegistus, or Mercurius ter Maximus, *i. e.* thrice greatest Intelligencer, because he was the first intelligencer who communicated celestial and divine knowledge to mankind by writing.

He was reported to have been king of Egypt; without doubt he was an Egyptian; nay, if you believe the Jews, even their Moses; and for the justification of this they urge, 1st, His being well skilled in *chemistry;* nay, the first who communicated that art to the sons of men; 2dly, They urge the *philosophic work, viz.* of rendering gold medicinal, or, finally, of the art of making *aurum potabile*; and, thirdly, of teaching the *Cabala*, which they say was shewn him by God on Mount Sinai : for all this is confessed to be originally written in Hebrew, which he would not have done had he not been an Hebrew, but rather in his vernacular tongue. But whether he was Moses or not *, it is certain he was an Egyptian, even as Moses himself also was; and therefore for the age he lived in, we shall not fall short of the time if we conclude he flourished much about the time of Moses; and if he really was not the identical Moses, affirmed to be so by many, it is more than probable that he was king of Egypt; for being chief philosopher, he was, according

---

* The Cabalists of the Hebrews affirm that Moses was this Hermes ; and although meek, yet was a man possessed of the most serious gravity, and a profound speculator in chemistry and divine magic ; that he by divine inspiration on the mount, became acquainted with the knowledge of all the natural and secret operations of nature ; that he taught the transmutation of metals *per Cabala, i. e.* by oral tradition, to the Jews.

to

to the Egyptian custom, initiated into the mysteries of priesthood, and from thence to the chief governor or king.

He was called Ter Maximus, as having a perfect knowledge of all things contained in the world (as his *Aureus*, or *Golden Tractate*, and his *Divine Pymander* shews,) which things he divided into three kingdoms, *viz.* animal, vegetable, and mineral; in the knowledge and comprehension of which three he excelled and transmitted to posterity, in *enigmas* and *symbols*, the profound secrets of nature; likewise a true description of the *Philosopher's Quintessence*, or *Universal Elixir*, which he made as the receptacle of all celestial and terrestrial virtues. The *Great Secret* of the philosophers he discoursed on, which was found engraven upon a Smaragdine table, in the valley of Ebron.

Johannes Functius, in his Chronology says, he lived in the time of Moses, twenty-one years before the law was given in the wilderness. Suidas seems to confirm it by saying, " Credo Mercurium Trismegistum sapientem Egyp-" tium floruisse ante Pharaonem." But this of Suidas may be applied to several ages, for that Pharaoh was the general name of their kings; or possibly it might be intended before the name of Pharaoh was given to their kings, which, if so *, he makes Trismegistus to exist 400 years before Moses, yea, before Abraham's descent into Egypt. There is no doubt but that he possessed the great secret of the philosophic work; and if God ever appeared in man, he appeared in him, as is evident both from his books and his Pymander; in which works he has communicated the sum of the abyss, and the divine knowledge to all posterity; by which he has demonstrated himself to have been not only an inspired divine, but also a deep philosopher, obtaining his wisdom from God and heavenly things, and not from man.

---

* According to the best authorities to be taken, Hermes Trismegistus lived in the time of Pharaoh, Israel's tyrant and oppressor, and was not the same with Moses who opposed Jannes and Jambres.

APPOL-

APPOLLONIUS OF TYANA,

WITH SOME ACCOUNT OF HIS

REMARKABLE MIRACLES, PROPHECIES, VISIONS, RELATIONS, &c. &c,

APPOLLONIUS Tyanæus, was one of the most extraordinary persons that ever appeared in the world.   He was born at Tyana in Cappadocia, towards the beginning of the first century.   At sixteen years of age he became a rigid disciple of Pythagoras, renouncing *wine, flesh*, and *women*, wearing no shoes, and letting his hair and beard grow long, and cloathing himself only in linen : soon after he became a reformer, and fixed his abode in a temple of Æsculapius, where many sick persons resorted to be cured by him.   Being come to age, he gave part of his estate to his eldest brother, and distributed another part to his poor relations, and kept back only a very small share to himself.   He lived six years without speaking a word, notwithstanding during this silence he quelled several seditions in Cecilia and Pamphilia ; that which he put a stop to at *Aspenda* was the most difficult of all to appease, because the business was to make those hearken to reason whom famine had driven to revolt : the cause of this commotion was, some rich men having monopolized all the corn, occasioned an extraordinary scarcity in the city ; *Appollonius* stopped this popular commotion, without speaking a word to the enraged multitude : Appollonius had no occasion for words ; his Pythagoric silence did all that the finest figures of oratory could effect.   He travelled much, professed himself a legislator ; understood all languages, without having learned them : he had the surprising faculty of knowing what was transacted at an immense distance, and at the time the Emperor Domitian was stabbed, Appollonius being at a vast distance, and standing in the market-place of the city, exclaimed, " Strike ! strike !—'tis done, the tyrant

is

is no more." He understood the language of birds; he condemned dancing, and other diversions of that sort; he recommended charity and piety; he travelled almost over all the countries of the world, and he died at a very great age. His life has been fully related by Philostratus; but it contains so many fabulous relations that we do not pretend to introduce them in this place. There are many who have very readily opposed the miracles of this man to those of Christ, and drew a parallel between them. It cannot be denied that this philosopher received very great honours, both during his life and after his death; and that his reputation continued long after paganism. He wrote four books of Judicial Astrology, and a Treatise on Sacrifices, shewing what was to be offered to the Deity.

' We must not omit a circumstance which tends to the honour of this ve-
' nerable person. It is related that *Aurelius* had come to a resolution, and
' had publikly declared his intentions, to demolish the city of *Tyana*; but
' that *Appollonius of Tyana*, an ancient philosopher, of great renown and au-
' thority, a true friend of the gods, and himself honoured as a deity, appear-
' ed to him in his usual form as he retired into his tent, and addressed him
' thus :—" *Aurelian*, if you desire to be victorious, think no more of the
" destruction of my fellow-citizens!—*Aurelian*, if you desire to rule, abstain
" from the blood of the innocent!—*Aurelian*, if you will conquer, be mer-
" ciful!" Aurelian being acquainted with the features of this ancient phi-
' losopher, having seen his image in several temples, he vowed to erect a
' temple and statues to him; and therefore altered his resolution of sacking
' *Tyana*. This account we have from men of credit, and have met with it
' in books in the Olpian library; and we are the more inclined to believe
' it on account of the dignity of *Appollonius*; for was there ever any thing
' among men more holy, venerable, noble, and divine than *Appollonius?*
' He restored life to the dead, he did and spoke many things beyond hu-
' man reach; which whoever would be informed of, may meet with many
' accounts of them in the Greek histories of his life.' See *Vopiscus in Au-*
relian, cap. 24.

Lastly,

Lastly, the inhabitants of *Tyana* built a temple to their *Appollonius* after his death; his statue was erected in several temples: the Emperor *Adrian* collected as many of his writings as he possibly could, and kept them very select, in his superb palace at *Antium*, with a rare but small book of this philosopher's, concerning the *Oracle of Trophonius*. This little book was to be seen at *Antium* during the life of Philostratus; nor did any curiosity whatever render this small town so famous as did this rare and extraordinary book of Appollonius.

It is reported that a wise prince of the Indians, well skilled in magic, made seven rings of the seven planets, which he bestowed upon Appollonius, one of which he wore every day; by which he always maintained the health and vigour of his youth, and lived to a very advanced age. His life was translated from the Greek of *Philostratus* into French, by *Blaise de Vigners*, with a very ample commentary by *Artus Thomas*, Lord of *Embry*, a *Parisian*; and some time since there has been made an English translation of his life, which was condemned, prohibited, and anathematized without reason.

PETRUS

PETRUS de ABANO, or PETER of APONA,

DOCTOR OF PHILOSOPHY AND PHYSIC, &c. &c. &c.

PETRUS APONENSIS, or Aponus, one of the most famous philosophers and physicians of his time, was born A. D. 1250, in a village, situated four miles from *Padua*. He studied a long time at *Paris*, where he was promoted to the degrees of Doctor in philosophy and physic, in the practice of which he was very successful, but his fees remarkably high. *Gabriel Naude*, in his *Antiquitate Scholæ Medicæ Parisiensis*, gives the following account of him : " Let us next produce Peter de Apona, or Peter de Abano, called the " Reconciler, on account of the famous book which he published during " his residence in your university *."—It is certain that physic lay buried in " Italy, scarce known to any one, uncultivated and unadorned, till its tutelar " genius, a villager of *Apona*, destined to free Italy from its barbarism and " ignorance, as Camillus once freed *Rome* from the siege of the *Gauls*, made " diligent enquiry in what part of the world polite literature was most happily " cultivated, philosophy most subtilly handled, and physic taught with the " greatest solidity and purity ; and being assured that *Paris* alone laid claim to " this honour, thither he presently flies ; giving himself up wholly to her tutelage, " he applied himself diligently to the mysteries of philosophy and medicine ; ob- " tained a degree and the laurel in both ; and afterwards taught them both with " great applause : and after a stay of many years, loaden with the wealth acquired " among you, and, after having become the most famous philosopher, astrologer, " physician, and mathematician of his time, returns to his own country, where,

---

* *Naude* takes notice of this in a speech in which he extols the ancient glory of the university of *Paris*. We have, above, recited his words at length, because they incidentally inform us, that Peter de Abano composed that great work at Paris which procured him the appellation of the *Reconciler*.

in

" in the opinion of the judicious *Scardeon,* he was the first restorer of true
" philosophy and physic. ˙Gratitude, therefore, calls upon you to acknowledge
" your obligations due to *Michæl Angelus Blondus,* a physician of *Rome,* who
" in the last century undertaking to publish the *Conciliationes Physiognomicæ*
" of your *Aponensian* doctor, and finding they had been composed at *Paris,*
" and in your university, chose to publish them in the name, and under the
" patronage, of your society." 'Tis said, that he was suspected of magic *,
and

---

* *Naude,* in his *Apology for great Men accused of Magic,* says, "The general opinion of almost all
" authors is, that he was the greatest magician of his time ; that by means of seven spirits, familiar, which
" he kept inclosed in chrystal, he had acquired the knowledge of the seven liberal arts, and that he had
" the art of causing the money he had made use of to return again into his pocket. He was accused of
" magic in the eightieth year of his age, and that dying in the year 1305, before his trial was over, he
" was condemned (as *Castellan* reports) to the fire ; and that a bundle of straw, or osier, representing his
" person, was publicly burnt at Padua ; that by so rigorous an example, and by the fear of incurring a
" like penalty, they might suppress the reading of three books which he had composed on this subject :
" the first of which is the noted *Heptameron,* or *Magical Elements of Peter de Abano, Philosopher,* now extant,
" and printed at the end of *Agrippa's* works ; the second, that which Trithemius calls *Elucidarium*
" *Necromanticum Petri de Abano* ; and a third, called by the same author *Liber experimentorum mirabilium*
" *de Annulis secundem,* 28 *Mansiom Lunæ."* Now it is to be noted, that Naude lays no stress upon these
seeming strong proofs ; he refutes them by immediately after affirming, that *Peter* of *Apona* was a man
of prodigious penetration and learning, living in an age of darkness which caused everything out of
the vulgar track to be suspected as diabolical, especially as he was very much given to study, and
acquainted with the harmony of the celestial bodies and the proportions of nature, and addicted to
curious and divinatory science. "He was one (says he) who appeared as a prodigy of learning amidst
" the ignorance of that age, and who, besides his skill in languages and physic, had carried his enquiries
" so far into the occult sciences of abstruse and hidden nature, that, after having given most ample
" proofs, by his writings concerning physiognomy, geomancy, and chiromancy, what he was able to
" perform in each of these, he quitted them all together with his youthful curiosity to addict himself
" wholly to the study of philosophy, physic, and astrology ; which studies proved so advantageous
" to him, that, not to speak of the two first, which introduced him to all the popes and sovereign pontiffs
" of his time, and acquired him the reputation which at present he enjoys among learned men, it
" is certain that he was a great master in the latter, which appears not only by the astronomical figures
" which he caused to be painted in the great hall of the palace at *Padua,* and the translations he made
" of the books of the most learned *Rabbi Abraham Aben Ezra,* added to those which he himself composed
" on *critical days,* and the improvement of astronomy, but by the testimony of the renowned mathema-
" tician *Regio Montanus,* who made a fine panegyric on him, in quality of an astrologer, in the oration
" which he delivered publicly at *Padua* when he explained there the book of *Alfraganus."* Now, many
respectable authors are of opinion that it was not on the score of magic that the Inquisition sentenced
him

and persecuted on that account by the Inquisition : and it is probable that, if he had lived to the end of his trial, he would have suffered in person what he was sentenced to suffer in effigy after his death. His apologists observe, that his body, being privately taken out of his grave by his friends, escaped the vigilance of the Inquisitors, who would have condemned it to be burnt. He was removed from place to place, and at last deposited in *St. Augustin's Church*, without Epitaph, or any other mark of honour. His accusers ascribed inconsistent opinions to him ; they charged him with being a magician, and yet with denying the existence of spirits. He had such an antipathy to milk, that the very seeing any one take it made him vomit. He died in the year 1316 * in the sixty-sixth year of his age. One of his principal books was the Conciliator, already mentioned.

him to death, but because he endeavoured to account for the wonderful effects in nature by the *influences of the celestial bodies*, not attributing them to *angels* or *dæmons* ; so that heresy, instead of magic, seems to have been the ground of his falling under the tyranny of the sage fathers of the Roman Catholic faith, as being one who *opposed* the doctrine of spiritual beings.

* If this be true as we read in *Tomasini*, in *Elog. Vilor. Illustr. p.* 22, *Naude* must be mistaken where he says, that " Peter Aponus being accused at the age of 80 years, died A.D. 1305." *Freherus* affirms the same upon the authority of *Bernardin Scardeon*. *Gesner* is mistaken in making Peter Aponus flourish in the year 1320. Konig has copied this error. But Father Rapin is much more grossly mistaken than any of them when he places him in the sixteenth century, saying, " *Peter of Apona*, a physician of *Padua*, " who flourished under Clement VII, debauched his imagination so far by reading the *Arabian* philoso- " phers, and by too much studying the astrology of Alfraganus, that he was put into the Inquisition " upon the suspicion of magic, &c." See *Rapin Reflex. sur la Philosophiæ, n.* 28, *p.* 360. *Vossius* has followed *Gesner*, and makes an observation worthy to be considered. He says, that *Peter of Apona* sent his book, *De Medicina Omnimoda*, to pope *John* XXII, who was elected in the year 1316, and held the *Pontifical Chair* seventeen years. By this we know the age of this physician. But if the year 1316 was that of his death, the conclusion is unjust ; neither does it clear *Vossius* of an error.

APULEIUS,

APULEIUS,

THE PLATONIC PHILOSOPHER.

———————

LUCIUS APULEIUS, a Platonic philosopher, publicly known by the famous work of the *Golden Ass,* lived in the second century under the Antonines. He was a native of *Madaura,* a *Roman* colony in *Africa*; his family was considerable; he had been well educated, and possessed a graceful exterior ; he had wit and learning; but was suspected of magic. He studied first at *Carthage,* then at *Athens,* and afterwards at *Rome,* where he acquired the Latin tongue without any assistance. An insatiable curiosity to know every thing induced him to make several voyages, and enter himself into several religious fraternities. He would see the bottom of their mysteries. He spent almost all his estate in travelling; insomuch, that being returned to *Rome,* and having a desire to dedicate himself to the service of *Osiris,* he lacked money to defray the expence of the ceremonies of his reception, he was obliged to make money of his clothes to complete the necessary sum : after this, he gained his living by pleading ; and, as he was eloquent and subtle, he did not want causes, some of which were very considerable. But he improved his fortunes much more by a lucky marriage than by pleading. A widow, whose name was Pudentilla, neither young nor fair, but who had a good estate, thought him worth her notice. He was not coy, nor was he solicitous to keep his fine person, his wit, his neatness, and his eloquence, for some young girl ; he married this rich widow chearfully (and with the most becoming philosophy overcame all turbulent passions, which might draw him into the snares of beauty,) at a country house near Oëa, a maritime town of Africa. This marriage drew upon him a troublesome law-suit. The relations of this lady's two sons urged that he had made use of art magic to possess himself of her

person

person and money; they accused him of being worse than a magician, *viz.* a wizard, before *Claudius Maximus*, Proconsul of *Africa*. He defended himself with great vigour *. His apology, which he delivered before the judges, furnishes

* Besides the accusation of magic, they reproached him with his beauty, his fine hair, his teeth, and his looking-glass. To the two first particulars he answered he was sorry their accusation was false.— "How do I wish," replied he, "that these heavy accusations of beauty, fine hair, &c. were just! I should, without difficulty, reply, as *Paris* in *Homer* does to Hector,

——————— *nor thou despise the charms*
With which a lover golden Venus arms.
Soft moving speech, and pleasing outward shew,
No wish can gain them, but the Gods bestow.
PObE.
POPE.

" Thus would I reply to the charge of beauty. Besides that, even philosophers are allowed to be of " a liberal aspect; that *Pythagoras*, the first of philosophers, was the handsomest man of his time; and " Zeno—but, as I observed, I am far from pretending to this apology; since, besides that nature has " bestowed but a very moderate degree of beauty on me, my continual application to study wears off " every bodily grace, and impairs my constitution. My hair, which I am falsely accused of curling " and dressing by way of ornament, is, as you see, far from being beautiful and delicate : on the contrary, " it is perplexed and entangled like a bundle of flocks or tow, and so knotty through long neglect of " combing, and even of disentangling, as never to be reduced to order." As to the third particular, he did not deny his having sent a very exquisite powder for the teeth to a friend, together with some verses, containing an exact description of the effects of the powder. He alleged that *all*, but especially those who spake in public, ought to be particularly careful to keep their mouths clean. This was a fine field for defence and for turning his adversary into ridicule; though, in all probability, he had given occasion enough for censure by too great an affectation of distinguishing himself from other learned men. Observe with how much ease some causes are defended, although the defendant be a little in the wrong. "I observed that some could scarce forbear laughing when our orator angrily accused me of " keeping my mouth clean, and pronounced the word tooth-powder with as much indignation as any one " ever pronounced the word poison. But, surely, it is not beneath a philosopher to study cleanliness, " and to let no part of the body be foul, or of an ill savour, especially the mouth, the use of which is " the most frequent and conspicuous, whether a man converses with another, or speaks in public, or says " his prayers in a temple. For speech is previous to every action of a man, and, as an excellent poet " says, proceeds from the Wall of the Teeth."

We may make the same observation upon the last head of his accusation. It is no crime in a doctor of what faculty soever, to have a looking-glass; but if he consults it too often in dressing himself, he is justly liable to censure. Morality in *Apuleius's* time was much stricter than at present as to external behaviour, for he durst not avow his making use of his looking-glass. He maintains that he *might* do it,

furnishes us with examples of the most shameful artifices that the villainy of
an impudent calumniator is capable of putting in practice *. Apuleius was
extremely laborious, and composed several books, some in verse and others in
prose, of which but a small part has resisted the injuries of time. He delighted
in making public speeches, in which he gained the applause of all his hearers.
When they heard him at Oëa, the audience cried out with one voice, that he

---

it, and proves it by several philosophical reasons, which, to say the truth, are much more ingenious than
judiciously applied ; but he denies that he ever consulted his looking-glass ; for he says, alluding to this
ludicrous accusation, " Next follows the long and bitter harangue about the looking-glass ; in which,
" so heinous is the crime, that *Pudens* almost burst himself with bawling out—' A philosopher to have
" a looking-glass !'—Suppose I should confess that I have, that you may not believe there is really some-
" thing in your objection, if I should deny it ; it does not follow from hence that I must necessarily
" make a practice of dressing myself at it. In many things I want the possession but enjoy the use of
" them. Now, if neither to have a thing be a proof that it is made use of, nor the want of it of the
" contrary, and as I am not blamed for possessing, but for making use of, a looking-glass, it is incum-
" bent upon him to prove farther at what time, and in what place, and in the presence of whom, I made
" use of it ; since you determine it to be a greater crime in a *philosopher* to see a looking-glass, than for
" the *profane* to behold the attire of *Ceres*."

    * I shall instance one to shew that in all ages the spirit of calumny has put men upon forging proofs
by false extracts from what a person has said or written. To convict Apuleius of practising magic, his
accusers alledge a letter which his wife had wrote during the time he paid his *devoirs* to her, and affirmed
that she had confessed, in *this letter*, that Apuleius was a *wizard*, and had actually bewitched her. It was
no hard matter to make the court believe that she had written so, for they only read a few words of her
letter, detached from what preceded or followed, and no one pressed them to read the whole. At last
Apuleius covered them with confusion by reciting the whole passage from his wife's letter. It appeared,
that far from complaining of Apuleius, she justified him, and artfully ridiculed his accusers. These
are his words : you will find that precisely the same terms may either condemn or justify *Apuleius*,
according as they are taken with or without what precedes them. " Being inclined to marry, for the
" reasons which I have mentioned, you yourself persuaded me to make choice of this man, being fond of
" him, and being desirous, by my means, to make him one of the family. But now, at the instigation of
" wicked men, *Apuleius* must be informed against as a magician (or wizard), and I, forsooth, am enchanted
" by him. I certainly love him : come to me before my reason fails me." He aggravates this kind
of fraud as it deserves ; his words deserve to be engraved in letters of gold, to deter (if possible) all
calumniators from practising the like cheats. He says, " There are many things which, produced
" alone, may seem liable to calumny. Any *discourse* may furnish matter of accusation, if what is con-
" nected with foregoing words be robbed of its introduction ; if some things be suppressed at pleasure,
" and if what is spoken by way of reproach to others, for inventing a calumny, be pronounced by the
" reader as an assertion of the truth of it."

ought

ought to be honoured with the freedom of the city. Those of Carthage heard him favourably, and erected a statue in honour of him. Several other cities did him the same honour. It is said that his wife held the candle to him whilst he studied; but this is not to be taken literally; it is rather a figure of Gallic eloquence in Sidonis Apollinaris, *Legentibus meditantibusque candelas & candelabra tenuerunt.* Several critics have published notes on Apuleius : witness *Phillipus Beraldus,* who published very large notes on the *Golden Ass,* at *Venice,* in folio, ann. 1504, which were reprinted in 8vo, at Paris, and at several other places. *Godescalk Stewichius, Peter Colvius, John Wiewer,* &c. have written on all the works of *Apuleius. Precius* published the *Golden Ass,* and the Apology, separately, with a great many observations. The annotations of *Casaubon,* and those of *Scipio Gentilis,* on the Apology, are very scarce, and much valued : the first appeared in the year 1594, and the latter in 1607. The *Golden Ass* may be considered (as Bayle says) as a continued satire on the disorders which the pseudo-magicians, priests, pandars, and thieves filled the world with at that time. This observation occurs in Fleuri's annotations. A person who would take the pains, and had the requisite qualifications, might draw up a very curious and instructive commentary on this romance, and might inform the world of several things which the preceding commentaries have never touched upon. There are some very obscene passages in this book of Apuleius. It is generally believed that this author has inserted some curious episodes in it of his own invention; and amongst others, that of *Psyche. Horum certe noster itæ-imitator fuit, ut è suo penu enumerabilia protulerit, atque inter cætera venustissimum illud Psyches,* Ἐπεισόδιον. This episode furnished *Moliere* with matter for an excellent Dramatic Piece, and *M. de la Fontaine* for a fine Romance.

ARISTOTLE,

ARISTOTLE,

THE PERIPATETIC.

ARISTOTLE, commonly called the Prince of Philosophers, or the Philosopher, by way of excellence, was the founder of a sect which surpassed, and at length even swallowed up all the rest. Not but that it has had reverse of fortune in its turn; especially in the seventeenth century, in which it has been violently shaken, though the Catholic divines on the one side, and the Protestant on the other, have run (as to the quenching of fire) to its relief, and fortified themselves so strongly, by the secular arm, against the New Philosophy, that it is not like to lose its dominion. Mr. *Moreri* met with so many good materials in a work of father Rapin, that he has given a very large article of Aristotle, enough to dispense with any assistance. Accordingly, I design not to enlarge upon it as far as the subject might allow, but shall content myself with observing some of the errors which I have collected concerning this philosopher. It is not certain that *Aristotle* practised pharmacy in *Athens* while he was a disciple of *Plato*, nor is it more certain that he did not. Very little credit ought to be given to a current tradition that he learnt several things of a *Jew*, and much less to a story of his pretended conversion to *Judaism*. They who pretend that he was born a *Jew*, are much more grossly mistaken: the wrong pointing of a certain passage occasioned this mistake. They are deceived who say that he was a disciple of *Socrates* for three years, for *Socrates* died 15 years before *Aristotle* was born. *Aristotle's* behaviour towards his master *Plato* is variously related: some will have it that, through prodigious vanity and ingratitude, he set up altar against altar: that is, he erected a school in *Athens* during *Plato's* life, and in opposition to him: others say that he did not set up for a professor till after his master's death. We are

told

told some things concerning his amours which are not altogether to his advantage. It was pretended that his conjugal affection was idolatrous, and that, if he had not retired from *Athens*, the process for irreligion, which the priests had commenced against him, would have been attended with the same consequences as that against *Socrates*. Though he deserved very great praise, yet it is certain that most of the errors concerning him are to be found in the extravagant commendations which have been heaped upon him : as, for example, is it not a downright falsehood to say, *that if Aristotle spoke in his natural philosophy like a man, he spoke in his moral philosophy like a God; and that it is a question in his moral philosophy whether he partakes more of the lawyer than of the priest; more of the priest than of the prophet; more of the prophet than of the God?* Cardinal *Pallavicini* scrupled not in some measure to affirm that, if it had not been for *Aristotle*, the church would have wanted some of its articles of faith. The Christians are not the only people who have authorized his philosophy; the *Mahometans* are little less prejudiced in its favour; and we are told, that to this day, notwithstanding the ignorance which reigns among them, they have schools for this sect. It will be an everlasting subject of wonder, to persons who know what philosophy is, to find that *Aristotle's* authority was so much respected in the schools, for several ages, that when a disputant quoted a passage from this philosopher, he who maintained the *thesis* durst nor say *transeat*, but must either deny the passage, or explain it in his own way. It is in this manner we treat the Holy Scriptures in the divinity schools. The parliaments which have proscribed all other philosophy but that of *Aristotle*, are more excusable than the doctors : for whether the members of parliament were really persuaded that this philosophy was the best of any, or was not, the public good might induce them to prohibit new opinions, lest the academical divisions should extend their malignant influence to the disturbance of the tranquillity of the state. What is most astonishing to wise men is, that the professors should be so strongly prejudiced in favour of *Aristotle's philosophy*. Had this prepossession been confined to his poetry and rhetoric, it had been less wonderful : but they were fond of the weakest

of

of his works; I mean his Logic, and Natural Philosophy *. This justice, however, must be done to the blindest of his followers, that they have deserted him where he clashes with Christianity; and this he did in points of the greatest consequence, since he maintained the eternity of the world, and did not believe that providence extended itself to sublunary beings. As to the immortality of the soul, it is not certainly known whether he acknowledged it or not †. In the year 1647, the famous capuchin, *Valerian Magni*, published a work concerning the Atheism of *Aristotle*. About one hundred and thirty years before, *Marc Antony Venerius* published a system of philosophy, in which he discovered several inconsistencies between *Aristotle's* doctrine, and the truths of religion. Campanella maintained the same in his book *de Reductione ad Religionem*, which was approved at *Rome* in the year 1630. It was not long since maintained in *Holland*, in the prefaces to some books, that the doctrine of this philosopher differed but little from Spinozism. In the mean time, if some Peripatetics may be believed, he was not ignorant of the mystery of the Trinity. He made a very good end, and enjoys eternal happiness. He composed a great number of books; a great part of which is come down to us. It is true some critics raise a thousand scruples about them. He was extremely honoured in his own city, and there were not wanting heretics who worshipped *his* image with that of *Christ*. There is extant some book which mentions, that, before the Reformation, there were churches in *Germany* in

---

* To be convinced of the weakness of these works, we need only read *Gassendus* in his *Exercitationes Paradoxicæ adversos Aristoteleos*. He says enough there against *Aristotle's* philosophy in general, to convince every unprejudiced reader that it is very defective; but he particularly ruins this philosopher's Logic. He was preparing, likewise, a criticism on his Natural Philosophy, his Metaphysics, and Ethics, in the same way; when, being alarmed at the formidable indignation of the *peripatetic* party against him, he chose rather to drop his work, than expose himself to their vexatious persecutions. In *Aristotle's* Logic and Natural Philosophy, there are many things which discover the elevation and profundity of his genius.

† *Pomponatius* and *Niphus* had a great quarrel on this subject. The first maintained, that the immortality of the soul was inconsistent with *Aristotle's* principles: the latter undertook to defend the contrary. See the discourse of la *Mothe le Vayer* on the Immortality of the Soul, and *Bodin*, in page 15 of Pref. to *Dæmonomania*.

which

which *Aristotle's* Ethics were read every *Sunday* morning to the people instead of the Gospel. There are but few instances of zeal for religion which have not been shewn for the *Peripatetic* philosophy. *Paul de Foix*, famous for his embassies and his learning, would not see *Francis Patricius* at *Ferrara*, because he was informed that that learned man taught a philosophy different from the *Peripatetic*. This was treating the enemies of *Aristotle* as *zealots* treat *heretics*. After all, it is no wonder that the *Peripatetic* philosophy, as it has been taught for several centuries, found so many protectors; or that the interests of it are believed to be inseparable from those of theology: for it accustoms the mind to acquiesce without evidence. This union of interests may be esteemed as a pledge to the *Peripatetics* of the immortality of their sect, and an argument to abate the hopes of the new philosophers.—Considering, withal, that there are some doctrines of Aristotle which the moderns have rejected, and which must, sooner or later, be adopted again. The Protestant divines have very much altered their conduct, if it is true, as we are told, that the first reformers clamoured so loud against the *Peripatetic* philosophy. The kind of death, which in some respects does much honour to the memory of *Aristotle*, is, that which some have reported, *viz.* that his vexation at not being able to discover the cause of the flux and reflux of the *Euripus* occasioned the distemper of which he died. Some say, that being retired into the island of *Eubœa*, to avoid a process against him for irreligion, he poisoned himself: but why should he quit *Athens* to free himself from persecution this way? HESYCHIUS affirms, not only that sentence of death was pronounced against him for an hymn which he made in honour of his father-in-law, but also that he swallowed aconite in execution of this sentence. If this were true, it would have been mentioned by more authors.

The number of ancient and modern writers who have exercised their pens on *Aristotle*, either in commenting on, or translating, him, is endless. A catalogue of them is to be met with in some of the editions of his works, but not a complete one. See a treatise of father Labbé, entitled *Aristotelis & Platonis Græcorum Interpretum, typis hactenus editorum brevis conspectus;* A short view of the Greek interpreters of Aristotle and Plato *hitherto published;*

printed

printed at *Paris* in the year 1657, in 4to.   Mr. *Teissier* names four authors who have composed the life of *Aristotle*; *Ammonius, Guarini of Verona, John James Beurerus*, and *Leonard Aretin*.   He forgot *Jerome Gemusæus*, physician and professor of philosophy at *Bazil*, author of a book, *De Vita Aristotelis, et ejus Operum Censura.—The Life of Aristotle, and a Critique on his Works.*

PETER BAYLE

ARTEMIDORUS OF EPHESUS,

THE

SOMNABULIST, OR DREAMER.

ARTEMIDORUS (who wrote so largely upon Dreams) was a native of *Ephesus*.   He lived under *Antonius Pius*, as he informs us himself, where he says, he knew an Athlete, who having dreamt that he had lost his sight, obtained the prize in the games which that Emperor ordered to be celebrated. No author has ever taken more pains upon so useful a subject than *Artemidorus* has done.   He bought up all that had been written upon the subject of dreams, which amounted to several volumes, but he spent many years in travelling to collect them, as well as the different opinions of all the learned who were then living.   He kept a continual correspondence with those in the towns and assemblies of Greece, in Italy, and in the most populous islands; and he collected every where all the dreams he could hear of, and the events they had.   He despised the censure of those grave and supercilious persons, who treat all pretenders to predictions as sharpers, or impostors, and without regarding the censures of these *Catos*, he frequented those diviners many years. In a word, he devoted all his time and thoughts to the science of dreams.   He

thought

thought that his great labour in making so many collections, &c. had enabled him to warrant his interpretations by reason and experience, but unfortunately he ever fixed upon the most trifling and frivolous subjects, such as almost every one is dreaming of: there is no dream which *Artemidorus* has explained, but will bear a quite different interpretation, with the same probability and with at least as natural resemblances, as those on which that interpreter proceeds. I say nothing of the injury done to *intelligences*, to whose direction we must necessarily impute our dreams if we expect to find in them any presage of futurity *. *Artemidorus* took great pains to instruct his son in the same science, as appears by the two books which he dedicated to him. So eager a pursuit after these studies is the less to be wondered at, when we consider that he believed himself under the inspiration of *Apollo*. He dedicated his three first

---

* We find in Artemidorus some of the most trifling incidents in dreams noted by him to presage very extraordinary things ; such, as if any one dreams of his nose, or his teeth, or such like trifling subjects, such particular events they must denote.—Now, as we cannot attribute a true and significant dream to any other cause than the celestial *intelligences*, or an *evil dæmon*, or else to the soul itself (which possesses an inherent prophetic virtue, as we have fully treated of in our *Second Book of Magic, where we have spoken of prophetic dreams*),—I say, from which of these causes a dream proceeds, we must ascribe but a very deficient portion of knowledge to either of them, if we do not allow them capable of giving better and plainer information respecting any calamity or change of fortune or circumstances, than by dreaming of one's nose itching, or a tooth falling out, and a hundred other toys like these.—I say, such modes of dictating to us a fore-knowledge of events to happen, cannot but be unworthy of their wisdom, subtilty, or power, and if they cannot instruct us by better signs, how great is their ignorance, and if they will not, how great is their malice? therefore, all such trifling dreams are to be altogether rejected as vain and insignificant, for we must remember that " *a dream comes through the multitude of business*," and often otherwise ; but such dreams as we are to notice, and draw predictions of future accidents and events, are those where the dream is altogether consistent, not depending upon any prior discourse, accidents, or other like circumstances ; likewise that the person who would wish to dream true dreams, should so dispose himself as to become a fit recipient of the heavenly powers, but this is only to be done by a temperate and frugal diet, a mind bent on sublime contemplation, a religious desire of being informed of any misfortune, accident, or event, which might introduce misery, poverty, or distraction of mind ; so as when we know it, to deprecate the same by prayer to the divine wisdom, that he would be pleased to divert the evil impending, or to enable us to meet the same with fortitude, and endure it with patience till the will of the Deity is accomplished. These are the things which we ought to be desirous to receive information of by *dream*, *vision*, or the like, and of which many are often truly forewarned, and thereby foretell things to come, also presage of the death of certain friends ; all which I know by experience to be true and probable.

books

books to one *Cassius Maximus*, and the other two to his son.—They were
printed in *Greek* at *Venice* in the year 1518. In the year 1603 *Rigaultius*
published them at *Paris* in *Greek* and *Latin*, with notes. The Latin translation he made use of was that published by *John Cornarius* at *Bazil*, in the
year 1539. *Artemidorus* wrote a treatise of *augury*, and another upon *chiromancy ;* but we have no remains of them. *Tertullian* has not taken notice of
him in that passage, where he quotes several *onirocritic* authors ; but *Lucian*
does not forget him, though he names but two writers of this class.

BABYLONIANS.

UNDER this article of *Babylonians* we shall just give the reader a general
sketch of the antiquity of occult learning among the Chaldeans of *Babylon*, so famous for their speculations in astrology. *Diodorus Siculus* informs
us, that the inhabitants of Babylon assert, that their city was very ancient ;
for they counted four hundred and seventy-three thousand years, from the first
observations of their astrologers to the coming of *Alexander*. Others say,
that the *Babylonians* boasted of having preserved in their archives the observations which their astrologers had made on nativities for the space of four
hundred and seventy thousand years ; from hence we ought to correct a passage of *Pliny*, which some authors make use of improperly, either to confute
the antiquity of Babylon, or for other purposes. Aristotle knew without
doubt that the *Babylonians* boasted of having a series of astronomical observations comprehending a prodigious number of centuries. He was desirous
to inform himself of the truth of this by means of *Calisthenes*, who was in
Alexander's retinue, but found a great mistake in the account ; for it is pretended that *Callisthenes* assured him that the astronomical observations he had

seen

seen in *Babylon*, comprehended no more than 1903 years. *Simplicius* reports this, and borrows it from *Porphyry*. If *Calisthenes* has computed right, it must be agreed, that after the deluge men made very great haste to become astrologers; for according to the Hebrew Bible there is but two thousand years * to be found from the flood to the death of *Alexander*. There is reason to question what *Simplicius* reports, and it is remarkable that all the ancient authors, who have ascribed the building of *Babylon* to *Semiramis*, have no authority than that of *Ctesias*, whose histories abounded in fables. And, therefore, we see that *Berosius* blames the *Greek* writers for affirming, that *Semiramis* built *Babylon*, and adorned it with the most beautiful structures. The supplement to *Moreri* quotes *Quintus Curtius*, in relation to the immo- desty of the *Babylonian* women †, who prostituted their bodies to strangers for money, under the idea of performing their devotions required by Venus. Observe, that these sums were afterwards applied to religious uses.

* *Epigenus* tells us, that amongst the Babylonians there were celestial observations for four hundred and seventy thousand years, inscribed on pillars or tables of bricks. *Berosius* and *Critodemus*, who make the least of it, say four hundred and ninety years.

† This lascivious ceremony was very ancient. *Jeremiah's* letter inserted in the book of *Baruch* touches something on it, but in an obscure manner, and wants a commentary taken out of *Herodotus*. Jeremiah's text runs thus :—" The women also with cords about them sat in the ways—but if any of them, drawn by " some that passeth by, lie with him, she reproacheth her fellow, that she was not thought as worthy as " herself, nor her cord broken."—Herodotus informs us, that there was a law in *Babylon* which obliged all the women of the country to seat themselves near the temple of *Venus*, and there to wait an opportunity of copulating with a stranger, &c. &c.

THE

THE LIFE

OF

HENRY CORNELIUS AGRIPPA, Knight,

DOCTOR OF BOTH LAWS, COUNSELLOR TO CHARLES V. EMPEROR OF GERMANY, AND
JUDGE OF THE PREROGATIVE COURT.

————

HENRY CORNELIUS AGRIPPA, a very learned man and a magician*, flourished in the sixteenth century. He was born at *Cologne* on the 14th of *September*, 1486. He descended from a noble and ancient family of Nettesheim in Belgia; desiring to walk in the steps of his ancestors, who for many generations had been employed by the princes of the house of *Austria*, he entered early into the service of the Emperor *Maximilian*. He had at first the employ of Secretary; but as he was equally qualified for the *sword* as the *pen*, he afterwards turned soldier, and served the Emperor seven years in his *Italian* army. He signalized himself on several occasions, and as a reward of his brave actions he was created *knight* in the field. He wished to add the academical honours to the military, he therefore commenced doctor of laws and physic. He was a man possessed of a very wonderful genius, and from his youth applied his mind to learning, and by his great natural talents he obtained great knowledge in almost all arts and sciences. He was a diligent searcher into the mysteries of nature, and was early in search of the philosopher's stone; and it appears that he had been recommended to some princes

* As he himself asserts in his preface to his three books of Occult Philosophy and Magic, where he says, "who am indeed a magician," applying the word magic to sublime and good sciences, not to prophane and devilish arts. *Paul Jovius, Thevet,* and *Martin del Rio,* accuse him not of *magic, (because we cannot apply that to necromantic arts)* but the *black art;* but we shall shew in some of the following notes, their grounds on which this accusation of *Agrippa* is founded, and examine how far their information will justify their calumny against this author.

as

as master of the art of alchymy *, and very fit for the grand projection. He had a very extensive knowledge of things in general, as likewise in the learned languages. He was pupil to *Trithemius*, who wrote upon the nature, ministry, and offices of intelligences and spirits. He was of an unsettled temper, and often changed his situation, and was so unfortunate as to draw upon himself the indignation of the Popish clergy by his writings. We find by his letters that he had been in *France* before the year 1507, that he travelled into *Spain* in the year 1508, and was at *Dole* in the year 1509. He read public lectures there, which engaged him in a contest with the *Cordelier Catilinet*. The monks in those times suspected whatever they did not understand, of heresy and error; how then could they suffer *Agrippa* to explain the mysterious works of *Reuchlinus de Verbo Mirifico* with impunity? It was the subject of the lectures which he read at *Dole* in 1509 with great reputation. To ingratiate himself the better with *Margaret of Austria*, governess of the *Austrian Netherlands*, he composed at that time a treatise on the excellency of women; but the persecution he suffered from the monks prevented him from publishing it; he gave up the cause, and came into *England*, where he wrote on *St. Paul's* Epistles, although he had another very private affair upon his hands. Being returned to *Cologne*, he read public lectures there on the questions of the divinity, which are called *Quodlibetales*; after which he went to the Emperor *Maximilian's* army in *Italy*, and continued there till Cardinal *de Sainte Croix* sent for him to *Pisa*. *Agrippa* would have displayed his abilities there in quality of theologist of the council, if that assembly had continued. This would not have been the way to please the Court of *Rome*, or to deserve the obliging letter he received from *Leo X*, and from whence we may conclude, that he altered his opinion. From that time he taught divinity publicly at *Pavia*, and at *Turin*. He likewise read lectures on *Mercurius Trismegistus* at *Pavia*, in the year 1515. He had a wife who was

---

* We have no authority to say, that ever he was in possession of the *great secret* of transmutation, neither can we gather any such information from his writings; the only circumstance relative to this is what himself says in occult philosophy, *that he had made gold, but no more than that out of which the soul was extracted.*

handsome

handsome and accomplished, by whom he had one son; he lost her in 1521; he married again an accomplished lady at Geneva in the year 1522, of whom he gives a very good character; by this wife he had three children, two sons and one daughter, who died. It appears by the second book of his letters, that his friends endeavoured in several places to procure him some honourable settlement, either at *Grenoble*, *Geneva*, *Avignon*, or *Metz*. He preferred the post which was offered him in this last city; and I find that in the year 1518 he was chosen by the lords of *Metz* to be their advocate, syndic, and orator. The persecutions which the monks raised against him, as well on account of his having refuted the common opinion concerning the three husbands of *St. Anne*, as because he had protected a country-woman, who was accused of witchcraft, made him leave the city of *Metz*. The story is as follows: —A country-woman, who was accused of witchcraft, was proposed (by the *Dominican*, *Nicholas Savini*, Inquisitor of the Faith at *Metz*) to be put to the torture, upon a mere prejudice, grounded on her being the daughter of a witch, who had been burnt. Agrippa immediately took up the cudgels, and did what he could to prevent so irregular a proceeding, but could not prevent the woman from being put to the *question*; however, he was the instrument of proving her innocence. Her accusers were condemned in a fine. The penalty was too mild, and far from a retaliation. This country-woman was of *Vapey*, a town situated near the gates of *Metz*, and belonging to the chapter of the cathedral. There appeared in *Messin*, who was the principal accuser of this woman, such sordid passions, and such a total ignorance of literature and philosophy, that *Agrippa*, in his letter of June 2, 1519, treats the town of Metz as—" *The stepmother of learning and virtue.*" This satyrical reflexion of Agrippa's might give rise to the proverb—" *Metz*, the covetous, and step-mother of arts and sciences."—What induced him to treat of the monogamy of *St. Anne* was his seeing, that *James Faber Stapulensis*, his friend, was pulled to pieces by the preachers of *Metz*, for having maintained that opinion. *Agrippa* retired to *Cologne*, his native city, in the year 1520, willingly forsaking a city, which the seditious inquisitors had made an enemy to learning and true merit. It is indeed the fate of all cities where such persons grow powerful of what-

soever

soever religion they are of. He again left his own city in the year 1521, and went to *Geneva*, but his fortunes did not much improve there, for he complained that he was not rich enough to make a journey to *Chamberi* to solicit the pension which he was led to expect from the Duke of *Savoy*. This expectation came to nothing, upon which *Agrippa* went from *Geneva* to *Fribourg* in *Switzerland* in the year 1523, to practise physic there as he had done at *Geneva*. The year following he went to *Lyons*, and obtained a pension from *Francis I*. He was in the service of that prince's mother in quality of her physician, but made no great improvement of his fortune there; neither did he follow that princess when she departed from *Lyons* in the month of *August*, 1525, to conduct her daughter to the frontiers of *Spain*. He danced attendance at *Lyons* for some time to employ the interest of his friends in vain, to obtain the payment of his pension; and before he received it he had the vexation to be informed that he was struck out of the list. The cause of this disgrace was, that having received orders from his mistress to enquire by the rules of astrology what turn the affairs of *France* would take, he expressed his disapprobation too freely, that the princess should employ him in such a vain curiosity, instead of making use of his abilities in more important affairs. The lady took this lesson very ill, but she was highly incensed when she heard that *Agrippa* had, by the *Rules of Astrology*, the *Cabala*, or some other art, predicted new triumphs to the constable of *Bourbon*.*—*Agrippa* finding himself

* See Agrippa's words in his 29th Epist. lib. iv. p. 854, which are as follow : — " I wrote to the " *Senechal*, desiring him to advise her not to misapply my abilities any longer in so unworthy an art ; " that I might for the future avoid these follies, since I had it in my power to be of service to her by " much happier studies." But the greatest misfortune was, that " *this unworthy art*," and " these follies,' " as he called them, predicted success to the opposite party, as you may judge by his own words.--" I re- " member I told the *Seneschal* in a letter, that in casting the constable of *Bourbon*'s nativity, I plainly " discovered that he would this year likewise gain the victory over your armies."—They who are acquainted with the history of these times, must see plainly that Agrippa could not pay his court worse to Francis I. than by promising good success to the constable. From that time Agrippa was looked upon as a *Bourbonist* : to silence this reproach he represented the service he had done to *France*, by dissuading 4000 foot soldiers from following the Emperor's party, and by engaging them in the service of *Francis I*. He alledged the refusal of the great advantages which were promised him when he left *Fribourg*, if he would enter into the constable's service. It appears by the 4th and 6th Letter of Book V. that he held

a strict

himself discarded, murmured, stormed, threatened, and wrote; but, however, he was obliged to look out for another settlement. He cast his eyes on the *Netherlands*, and having after long waiting obtained the necessary passes, he arrived at *Antwerp* in the month of *July*, 1528. One of the causes of these delays was the rough proceeding of the Duke of *Vendôme*, who instead of signing the pass for *Agrippa* tore it up, saying, that " he would not sign any passport for a conjuror." In the year 1529 the King of *England* sent *Agrippa* a kind invitation to come into his territories, and at the same time he was invited by the Emperor's chancellor, by an *Italian* marquiss, and by *Margaret* of *Austria*, governess of the *Netherlands*. He accepted the offers of the latter, and was made historiographer to the Emperor, a post procured him by that princess. He published by way of prelude, *The History of the Government of Charles V.* and soon after he was obliged to compose that princess's funeral oration, whose death was in some manner the life of our *Agrippa*; for she had been strangely prejudiced against him: the same ill office was done him with his Imperial Majesty. His treatise of *the Vanity of the Sciences*, which he caused to be printed in 1530, terribly exasperated his enemies. That which he published soon after at *Antwerp*, viz. *of the Occult Philosophy*, afforded them a still farther pretence to defame him. It was fortunate for him that Cardinal *Campegius*, the Pope's legate, and Cardinal *De la Mark*, Bishop of *Liege*, were his advocates; but, however, their good offices could not procure him his pension as historiographer, nor prevent his being imprisoned at *Brussels*, in the year 1531, but he was soon released. The following year he made a visit to the Archbishop of Cologne, to whom he had dedicated his *Occult Philosophy*, and from whom he had received a very obliging letter. The fear of his creditors, with whom he was much embarrassed on account of his salary being stopped, made him stay longer in the country of *Cologne* than he desired. He strenuously opposed the inquisitors, who had put a stop to the printing of his *Occult Philosophy*,

a strict correspondence with that prince in 1527. He advised and counselled, yet refused to go and join him, and promised him victory. He assured him that the walls of Rome would fall down upon the first attack; yet he omitted informing him of one point, and that was, that the constable would be killed there.

when

when he was publishing a new edition of it corrected, and augmented at Cologne.—See the xxvith, and the following Letters of the viith Book. In spite of them the impression was finished, which is that of the year 1533. He continued at *Bonn* till the year 1535, and was then desirous of returning to *Lyons.* He was imprisoned in *France* for something he had said against the mother of Francis I. but was released at the request of certain persons, and went to *Grenoble*, where he died the same year, 1535. Some say that he died in the hospital (but this is mere malice, for his enemies reported every thing that envy could suggest to depreciate his worth and character). *He died at the house of the Receiver General of the province of* Dauphiny, *whose son was* first president *of Grenoble.* Mr. *Allard*, at p. 4, *of the Bibliotheque of Dauphiné,* says, that *Agrippa* died at *Grenoble, in the house which belonged to the family of* Ferrand *in Clerk's Street, and was then in the possession of the president* Vachon ; *and that he was buried in the convent of the* Dominicans. He lived always in the *Roman* communion, therefore it ought not to have been said that he was a Lutheran *. Burnet in his history of the Reformation asserts, that *Agrippa* wrote in favour of the divorce of King *Henry* VIII. But if we look into *Agrippa's* letters we shall find that he was against it, as well in them as likewise in his declamation on the vanity of the sciences, where he says---" I am informed there is a certain " king, at this time o'day, who thinks it lawful for him to divorce a wife to " whom he has been married these twenty years, and to espouse an harlot." In respect of the charge of magic diabolical being preferred against him by *Martin del Rio* and others who confidently asserted, that *Agrippa* paid his way at inns, *&c.* with pieces of horn, casting an illusion over the senses, whereby those who received them took them for real money ; together with the story of the boarder at *Louvain*, who, in *Agrippa's* absence, raised the devil in his study, and thereby lost his life ; and *Agrippa's* coming home, and seeing the spirits dancing at the top of the house, his commanding one of them into the dead body, and sending it to drop down at the market-place : all these stories, asserted

* *Agrippa, in his Apolog. cap.* 19, speaks in lofty terms of *Luther*, and with such contempt of the adversaries of that reformer that it is plain from hence *Sixtus Sienensis* affirmed that *Agrippa* was a Lutheran.

by

by *Martin del Rio*, are too ridiculous to be believed by men of sense or science, they being no way probable even if he had dealt in the Black Art.—As to *magic*, in the sense it is understood by us, there is no doubt of his being a proficient in it, witness his three books of Occult Philosophy ; to say nothing here of the fourth, which we have good authority to say was never wrote by *Agrippa*, as we shall shew presently, where we shall treat of the history of his *Occult Philosophy.*—In a word, to sum up the character of Agrippa we must do him the justice to acknowledge, that notwithstanding his impetuous temper which occasioned him many broils, yet from the letters which he wrote to several of his most intimate friends, without any apparent design of printing them, he was a man used to religious reflexions, and the practice of Christianity ; that he was well versed in many of the chiefest and most secret operations of nature, *viz.* the sciences of natural and celestial magic ; that he certainly performed strange things (in the vulgar eye) by the application of *actives* to *passives*, as which of us cannot ? that he was an expert *astrologer*, *physician*, and *mathematician*, by which, as well as by magic, he foretold many uncommon things, and performed many admirable operations. *John Wierus*, who was his domestic, has given several curious and interesting anecdotes which throw great light upon the mysterious character of *Agrippa*, and serve to free him from the scandalous imputation of his being a professor of the BLACK ART. Now, because *Agrippa* continued whole weeks in his study, and yet was acquainted with almost every transaction in several countries of the world, many silly people gave out, that a black dog which *Agrippa* kept was an evil spirit, by whose means he had all this information, and which communicated the *enemies' posts, number, designs, &c.* to his master ; this is *Paul Jovius's* account, by which you may see on what sort of reports he founded his opinions of this great man. We wonder that *Gabriel Naudé* had not the precaution to object to the accusers of *Agrippa*, the great number of historical falsehoods of which they (his accusers) stand convicted. *Naudé* supposes that the monks and others of the ecclesiastical order did not think of crying down the *Occult Philosophy* till a long time after it was published ; he affirms that they exclaimed against that work, only in revenge for the injuries

they

they believed they had received in that of the *Vanity of the Sciences*. 'Tis true, this latter book gave great offence to many. The monks, the members of the universities, the preachers, and the divines, saw themselves drawn to the life in it. *Agrippa* was of too warm a complexion. " *The least taste of his book* (of the Vanity of the Sciences) *convinced me that he was an author of a fiery genius, extensive reading, and great memory ; but sometimes more copious than choice in his subject, and writing in a disturbed, rather than in a composed, style.*" He lashes vice, and commends virtue, every where, and in every person : but there are some with whom nothing but panegyric will go down. *See* ERASMI Epist. *lib.* xxvii. *p.* 1083.

Let us now, in a few words, and for the conclusion of this article, describe the history of the *Occult Philosophy*. *Agrippa* composed this work in his younger days, and shewed it to the Abbot *Trithemius*, whose pupil he had been. Trithemius was charmed with it, as appears by the letter which he wrote to him on the 8th of *April*, 1510; but he advises him to communicate it only to those whom he could confide in. However, several manuscript copies of it were dispersed almost all over *Europe*. It is not necessary to observe that most of them were faulty, which never fails to happen in the like cases. They were preparing to print it from one of these bad copies ; which made the author resolve to publish it himself, with the additions and alterations with which he had embellished it, after having shewed it to the Abbot *Trithemius*. *Melchior Adam* was mistaken in asserting that *Agrippa*, in his more advanced years, having corrected and enlarged this work, shewed it to the Abbot *Trithemius*. He had refuted his *Occult Philosophy* in his *Vanity of the Sciences*, and yet he published it to prevent others from printing a faulty and mutilated edition. He obtained the approbation of the doctors of divinity, and some other persons, whom the Emperor's council appointed to examine it.

" *This book has been lately examined and approved by certain prelates of the*
" *church, and doctors, thoroughly versed both in sacred and profane literature,*
" *and by commissaries particularly deputed for that purpose by* CÆSAR'S *council :*
" *after which, it was admitted by the whole council, and licensed by the authentic*
diploma

" *diploma of his Imperial Majesty, and the stamp of the* Cæsarean *Eagle in*
" *red wax; and was afterwards publicly printed and sold at* Antwerp, *and*
" *then at* Paris, *without any opposition.*"

After the death of *Agrippa* a *Fourth Book* was added to it by another hand.
Jo. Wierus de Magis, cap. 5. p. 108, says, " *To these* (books of Magic)
" *may very justly be added, a work lately published, aud ascribed to my late*
" *honoured host and preceptor,* Henry Cornelius Agrippa, *who has been*
" *dead more than forty years; whence I conclude it is unjustly inscribed to his*
" *manes, under the title of* The Fourth book of the Occult Philosophy,
" or of Magical Ceremonies, *which pretends likewise to be a Key to the*
" *three former books of the* Occult Philosophy, *and all kinds of Magical*
" *Operations.*" Thus John Wierus expresses himself. There is an edition
in folio of the *Occult Philosophy,* in 1533, without the place where it was
printed. The privilege of *Charles V.* is prefixed to it, dated from *Mechlin,*
the 12th of *January,* 1529. We have already mentioned the chief works of
Agrippa. It will be sufficient to add, that he wrote *A Commentary on the Art
of Raimundus Lullius* and *A Dissertation on the Original of Sin,* wherein he
teaches that the fall of our first parents proceeded from their unchaste love.
He promised a work against the *Dominicans,* which would have pleased many
persons both within and without the pale of the church of *Rome*.* He held
some uncommon opinions, and never any Protestant spoke more forcibly against
the impudence of the Legendaries, than he did. We must not forget the Key
of his *Occult Philosophy,* which he kept only for his friends of the first rank,
and explained it in a manner, which differs but little from the speculations of
our Quietists. Now many suppose that the 4th book of the *Occult Philosophy*
is the Key which Agrippa mentions in his letters to have reserved to himself;
but it may be answered, with great shew of probability, that he amused the

---

* "In the treatise I am composing of the vices and erroneous opinions of the *Dominicus,* in which
" I shall expose to the whole world their vicious practices, such as the sacrament often infected with
" poison—numberless pretended miracles—kings and princes taken off with poison—cities and states
" betrayed—the populace seduced—heresies avowed—and the rest of the deeds of these heroes and their
" enormous crimes." See Agrippa *Opera,* T. ii. p. 1037.

world

world with this Key to cause himself to be courted by the curious. *James Gohory* and *Vigenere* say, that he pretended to be master of the Practice of the Mirror of *Pythagoras*, and the secret of extracting the spirit of gold from its body, in order to convert silver and copper into fine gold. But he explains what he means by this Key, where he says, in the Epist. 19. lib. v. "*This* "*is that true and occult philosophy of the wonders of nature. The key thereof* "*is the understanding : for the higher we carry our knowledge, the more sublime* "*are our attainments in virtue, and we perform the greatest things with more ease* "*and effect.*" Agrippa makes mention of this Key in two letters which he wrote to a religious who addicted himself to the study of the *Occult Sciences*, *viz. Aurelius de Aquapendente Austin*, friar, where he says, "*What surprising* "*accounts we meet with, and how great writings there are made of the invincible* "*power of the* Magic Art, *of the prodigious images of* Astrologers, *of the amazing* "*transmutations of* Alchymists, *and of that blessed stone by which*, MIDAS-*like*, "*all metals are transmuted into gold: all which are found to be vain, fictitious,* "*and false, as often as they are practised literally.*" Yet he says, "Such things "are delivered and writ by great and grave philosophers, whose traditions who "dare say are false? Nay, it were impious to think them lies : only there is "another meaning than what is writ with the bare letters. We must not, *he adds*, "look for the principle of these grand operations without ourselves : it is an "internal spirit within us, which can very well perform whatsoever the "monstrous *Mathematicians*, the prodigious *Magicians*, the wonderful *Al-* "*chymists*, and the bewitching *Necromancers*, can effect."

Nos habitat, non tartara ; sed nec sidera cœli,
Spiritus in nobis qui viget, illa facit.

See AGRIPPA *Epist. dat. Lyons, Sept.* 24, 1727.

Note. Agrippa's three books of Magic, with the fourth, were translated into English, and published in London in the year 1651. But they are now become so scarce, as very rarely to be met with, and are sold at a very high price by the booksellers.

ALBERTUS

ALBERTUS MAGNUS.

ALBERTUS MAGNUS, a *Dominican*, bishop of *Ratisbon*, and one of the most famous doctors of the XIII century, was born at *Lawingen*, on the *Danube*, in *Suabia*, in the year 1193, or 1205. *Moreri's* dictionary gives us an account of the several employs which were conferred upon him, and the success of his lectures in several towns. It is likewise said, that he practised midwifery, and that he was in search of the *Philosopher's Stone :* that he was a famous *Magician*, and that he had formed a machine in the shape of a man, which served him for an oracle, and explained all the difficulties which he proposed to it. I can easily be induced to believe that, as he understood the mathematics, *&c.* he made a head, which, by the help of some spirits, might form certain articulate sounds. Though he was well qualified to be the inventor of artillery, there is reason to believe, that they who ascribed the invention of it to him are mistaken. It is said that he had naturally a very dull wit, and that he was upon the point of leaving the cloister, because he despaired of attaining what his friar's habit required of him, but that the Holy Virgin appeared to him, and asked him in which he would chuse to excel, in philosophy or divinity ; that he made choice of philosophy, and that the Holy Virgin told him he should surpass all men of his time in that science, but that, as a punishment for not chusing divinity, he should before his death, relapse into his former stupidity. They add, that, after this apparition, he shewed a prodigious deal of sense, and so improved in all the sciences, that he quickly surpassed his preceptors ; but that, three years before his death, he forgot in an instant all that he knew : and that, being at a stand in the middle of a lecture on divinity at *Cologne*, and endeavouring in vain to recal his ideas, he

was

was sensible that it was the accomplishment of the prediction. Whence arose the saying, that he was miraculously converted from an ass into a philosopher, and, afterwards, from a philosopher into an ass. Our Albertus was a very little man*, and, after living eighty-seven years, died in the year of our redemption, 1280, at *Cologne*, on the 15th of November; his body was laid in the middle quire of the convent of the *Dominicans*, and his entrails were carried to *Ratisbon;* his body was yet entire in the time of the *Emperor. Charles V.* and was taken up by his command, and afterwards replaced in its first monument. He wrote such a vast number of books, that they amount to twenty-one volumes in folio, in the edition of *Lyons*, 1651.

ROGER BACON,

COMMONLY CALLED

FRIAR BACON.

ROGER BACON, an Englishman, and a *Franciscan* friar, lived in the XIII century. He was a great *Astrologer, Chymist, Mathematician,* and *Magician.* There runs a tradition in English annals, that this friar made a brazen head, under the rising of the planet Saturn, which spake with a man's voice, and gave responses to all his questions. *Francis Picus* says, " that he read " in a book wrote by Bacon, that a man might foretel things to come by means " of the mirror *Almuchesi*, composed according to the rules of perspective ; pro- " vided he made use of it under a good constellation, and first brought his body " into an even and temperate state by chymistry." This is agreeable to what *John Picus* has maintained, that *Bacon* gave himself only to the study of *Natural Magic.* This friar sent several instruments of his own invention to pope Clement IV. Several of his books have been published (but they are now very

---

* When he came before the Pope, after standing some time in his presence, his Holiness desired him to rise, thinking he had been kneeling.

scarce)

scarce,) *viz. Specula Mathematica & Perspectiva, Speculum Alchymiæ, De Mirabili Potestate Artis & Naturæ, Epistolæ, cum Notis, &c.* In all probability he did not perform any thing by any compact with devils, but has only ascribed to things a surprising efficacy which they could not naturally have. He was well versed in judicial astrology. His Speculum Astrologiæ was condemned by Gerson and Agrippa. Francis Picus and many others have condemned it only because the author maintains in it, *that, with submission to better judgments, books of magic ought to be carefully preserved, because the time draws near that, for certain causes not there specified, they must necessarily be perused and made use of on some occasions.* *Naude* adds, " that *Bacon* was so much addicted to judicial astrology, that *Henry de Hassia, William* of *Paris*, and *Nicholas Oresmius*, were obliged to inveigh sharply against his writings." *Bacon* was fellow of *Brazen-nose* college in *Oxford* in the year 1226. He was beyond all compeer the glory of the age he lived in, and may perhaps stand in competition with the greatest that have appeared since. It is wonderful, considering the age wherein he lived, how he came by such a depth of knowledge on all subjects. His treatises are composed with that elegancy, conciseness, and strength, and abound with such just and exquisite observations on nature, that, among the whole line of chymists, we do not know one that can pretend to contend with him. The reputation of his uncommon learning still survives in *England*. His cell is shewn at *Oxford* to this day ; and there is a tradition, that it will fall whenever a greater man than *Bacon* shall enter within it. He wrote many treatises ; amongst which, such as are yet extant have beauties enough to make us sensible of the great loss of the rest. What relates to chymistry are two small pieces, wrote at *Oxford*, which are now in print, and the manuscripts to be seen in the public library at *Leiden ;* having been carried thither among *Vossius's* manuscripts from *England*. In these treatises he clearly shews how imperfect metals may be ripened into perfect ones. He entirely adopts *Geber's* notion, that mercury is the common basis of all metals, and sulphur the cement ; and shews that it is by a gradual depuration of the mercurial matter by sublimation, and the accession of a subtle sulphur by fire, that nature makes her gold ; and that, if during the process, any other third matter happen to

intervene,

intervene, besides the mercury and sulphur, some base metal arises : so that, if we by imitating her operations ripen lead, we might easily change it into good gold.

Several of *Bacon's* operations have been compared with the experiments of Monsieur *Homberg*, made by that curious prince the duke of *Orleans;* by which it has been found that *Bacon* has described some of the very things which *Homberg* published as his own discoveries. For instance, *Bacon* teaches expressly, that if a pure sulphur be united with mercury, it will commence gold : on which very principle, Monsieur *Homberg* has made various experiments for the production of gold, described in the *Memoire de l'Academie Royale des Sciences.* His other physical writings shew no less genius and force of mind. In a treatise * *Of the secrets Works of Nature*, he shews that a person who was perfectly acquainted with the manner nature observes in her operations, would not only be able to rival, but to surpass nature herself.

This author's works are printed in 8vo and 12mo, under the title of *Frater Rogerius Baco de Secretis Artis & Naturæ*, but they are become very rare. From a repeated perusal of them we may perceive that *Bacon* was no stranger to many of the capital discoveries of the present and past ages. Gunpowder he certainly knew; thunder and lightning, he tells us, may be produced by art ; and that sulphur, nitre, and charcoal, which when separate have no sensible effect, when mingled together in a due proportion, and closely confined, yield a horrible crack. A more precise description of gunpowder cannot be given with words : and yet a Jesuit, *Barthol. Schwartz*, some ages afterwards, has had the honour of the discovery. He likewise mentions a sort of inextinguishable fire, prepared by art, which indicates he knew something of phosphorus. And that he had a notion of the rarefaction of the air, and the structure of the air-pump, is past contradiction. A chariot, he observes, might be framed on the principle of mechanics, which, being sustained on very large globes, specifically lighter than common air, would carry a man aloft through the atmosphere; this proves that he likewise had a competent idea of aerostation.

* De Secretis Naturæ Operibus.

There

There are many curious speculations in this noble author, which will raise the admiration of the reader : but none of them will affect him with so much wonder, as to see a person of the most sublime merit fall a sacrifice to the wanton zeal of infatuated bigots.   See BOERHAAVE'S *Chym.* p. 18.

RAYMOND LULLY,

A FAMOUS ALCHYMIST.

RAYMOND LULLY, or *Raymon Lull,* comes the next in order.   He was born in the island of *Majorca,* in the year 1225, of a family of the first distinction, though he did not assume his chymical character till towards the latter part of his life.

Upon his applying himself to chymistry, he soon began to preach another sort of doctrine; insomuch that, speaking of that art, he says it is only to be acquired by dint of experiment and practice, and cannot be conveyed to the understanding by idle words and sounds.   He is the first author I can find, who considers alchymy expressly with a view to the universal medicine : but after him it became a popular pursuit, and the libraries were full of writings in that vein.

Lully, himself, beside what he wrote in the scholastic way, has a good many volumes wrote after his conversion : 'tis difficult to say how many; for it was a common practice with his disciples and followers to usher in their perform-ances under their master's name.   " I have perused (*says Boerhaave)* the best
" part of his works, and find them, beyond expectation, excellent : insomuch,
" that I have been almost tempted to doubt whether they could be the work
" of that age, so full are they of the experiments and observations which
" occur in our later writers, that either the books must be supposititious, or else
" the

" the ancient chymists must have been acquainted with a world of things which
" pass for the discoveries of modern practice. He gives very plain intimations
" of phosphorus, which he calls the *Vestal Fire*, the *Offa Helmontii, &c.* and
" yet it is certain he wrote 200 years before either *Helmont,* or my Lord
" *Bacon.*"

He travelled into *Mauritania,* where he is supposed to have first met with
chymistry, and to have imbibed the principles of his art from the writings of
Geber : which opinion is countenanced by the conformity observable between
the two. The *Spanish* authors ascribe the occasion of his journey to an amour :
he had fallen in love, it seems, with a maiden of that country, who obstinately
refused his addresses. Upon enquiring into the reason, she shewed him a can-
cered breast. *Lully,* like a generous gallant, immediately resolved on a voyage
to *Mauritania,* where *Geber* had lived, to seek some relief for his mistress. He
ended his days in *Africa ;* where, after having taken up the quality of mission-
ary, and preaching the gospel among the infidels, he was stoned to death *.

* The history of this eminent adept is very confused. *Mutius,* an author, is express, that that good man,
being wholly intent upon religion, never applied himself either to chymistry or the philosopher's-stone :
and yet we have various accounts of his making gold. Among a variety of authors, *Gregory* of *Thoulouse*
asserts that *"Lully offered* EDWARD III. *king of England, a supply of six millions to make war against the
Infidels."* Besides manuscripts, the following printed pieces bear *Lully's* name, *viz. The Theory of the
Philosopher's Stone : The Practise : The Transmutation of Metals : The Codicil : The Vade-Mecum : The
Book of Experiments : The Explanation of his Testament : The Abridgements, or Accusations : and The
Power of Riches.*

GEORGE

GEORGE RIPLEY.

GEORGE RIPLEY, an *Englishman* by nation, and by profession a canon
or monk of *Britlingthon*.   His writings were all very good in their kind,
being wrote exactly in the style of *Bacon*, only more allegorical.   As he was no
physician, he does not meddle with any thing of the preparations of that kind;
but treats much of the cure of metals, which in his language is the purification
and maturation thereof.   He rigorously pursued *Geber*'s and *Bacon*'s principles,
and maintained, for instance, with new evidence, that mercury is the universal
matter of all metals; that this set over the fire, with the purest sulphur, will
become gold, but that if either of them be sick or leprous, *i. e.* infected with
any impurity, instead of gold, some other metal will be produced.   He adds,
that as mercury and sulphur are sufficient for the making of all metals : so of
these may an universal medicine, or metal, be produced for curing of all the
sick; which some mistakenly understood of an universal metal, efficacious in
all the diseases of the human body.

JOHN, AND ISAAC HOLLANDUS.

THEY were two brothers, both of them of great parts and ingenuity,
and wrote on the dry topics of chymistry.   They lived in the 13th century,
but this is not assured.   The whole art of *enamelling* is their invention, as
is also, that of *colouring glass*, and precious stones, by application of thin metal
plates.

plates. Their writings are in the form of processes, and they describe all their operations to the most minute circumstances. The treatise of *enamelling* is esteemed the greatest and most finished part of their works : whatever relates to the fusion, separation, and preparation of metals, is here delivered. They write excellently of *distillation, fermentation, putrefaction,* and their effects ; and seem to have understood, at least, as much of these matters as any of the moderns have done. They furnish a great many experiments on human blood ; which *Van Helmont* and Mr. *Boyle* have since taken for new discoveries. I have a very large work in folio, under their name, of the construction of chymical furnaces and instruments. Their writings are as easily purchased, as they are worthy of perusal, on account of valuable secrets in them, which may pave the way for greater discoveries. See BOERHAAVE, p. 21.

PHILIPPUS

PHILIPPUS AUREOLUS THEOPHRASTUS PARACELSUS BOMBAST DE HOENHEYM,

THE PRINCE OF PHYSICIANS AND PHILOSOPHERS BY FIRE;
GRAND PARADOXICAL PHYSICIAN;
THE TRISMEGISTUS OF SWITZERLAND;
FIRST REFORMER OF CHYMICAL PHILOSOPHY;
ADEPT IN ALCHYMY, CABALA, AND MAGIC;
NATURE'S FAITHFUL SECRETARY;
MASTER OF THE ELIXIR OF LIFE AND THE PHILOSOPHER'S STONE;

AND THE

GREAT MONARCH OF CHYMICAL SECRETS;

Now living in his Tomb, whither he retired disgusted with the Vices and Follies of Mankind, supporting himself with his own

QUINTESSENTIA VITÆ.

————————

PARACELSUS was born, as he himself writes, in the year 1494, in a village in *Switzerland* called Hoenheym (q. d. *ab alto nido*) two miles distant from *Zurich*. His father was a natural son of a great master of the *Teutonic* order, and had been brought up to medicine, which he practised accordingly in that obscure corner. He was master of an excellent and copious library, and is said to have become eminent in his art, so that *Paracelsus* always speaks of him with the highest deference, and calls him *laudatissimus medicus in eo vico*. Of such a father did *Paracelsus* receive his first discipline. After a little course of study at home he was committed to the care of *Trithemius*, the celebrated abbot of *Spanheim*, who had the character of an adept himself, and wrote of the *Cabala*, being at that time a reputed *magician*. Here he chiefly learnt languages and letters; after which he was removed to *Sigismund Fugger* to learn medicine, surgery, and chymistry; all these masters, especially the

the last, *Paracelsus* ever speaks of with great veneration; so that he was not altogether so rude and unpolished as is generally imagined. Thus much we learn from his own writings, and especially the preface to his *Lesser Surgery*, where he defends himself against his accusers. At twenty years of age he undertook a journey through *Germany* and *Hungary*, visiting all the mines of principal note, and contracting an acquaintance with the miners and workmen, by which means he learnt every thing relative to metals, and the art thereof : in this enquiry he shewed an uncommon assiduity and resolution. He gives us an account of the many dangers he had run from earthquakes, falls of stones, floods of water, cataracts, exhalations, damps, heat, hunger, and thirst; and every where takes occasion to insist on the value of an art acquired on such hard terms. The same inclination carried him as far as *Muscovy*, where as he was in quest of mines near the frontiers of *Tartary* he was taken prisoner by that people, and carried before the great *Cham*; during his captivity there he learnt various secrets, till, upon the Cham's sending an embassy to the Grand Signior, with his own son at the head of it, *Paracelsus* was sent along with him in quality of companion. On this occasion he came to *Constantinople* in the twenty-eighth year of his age, and was there taught the secret of the *philosopher's stone* by a generous *Arabian*, who made him this noble present, as he calls it, *Azoth*. This incident we have from *Helmont* only; for *Paracelsus* himself, who is ample enough on his other travels, says nothing of his captivity. At his return from *Turkey* he practised as a surgeon in the Imperial army, and performed many excellent cures therein; indeed, it cannot be denied but that he was excellent in that art, of which his *great surgery*, printed in folio, will ever be a standing monument. At his return to his native country he assumed the title of *utriusque medicinæ doctor*, or doctor both of external and internal medicine or surgery; and grew famous in both, performing far beyond what the practice of that time could pretend to; and no wonder, for medicine was then in a poor condition; the practice and the very language was all *Galenical* and *Arabic*; nothing was inculcated but *Aristotle*, *Galen*, and the *Arabs*; Hippocrates was not read; nay, there was no edition of his writings, and scarce was he ever mentioned. Their theory consisted

consisted in the knowledge of the four degrees, the temperaments, &c. and their whole practice was confined to venesection, purgation, vomiting, clysmata, &c. Now, in this age a new disease had broke out, and spread itself over *Europe*, *viz.* the *venereal disorder*; the common *Galenic* medicines had here proved altogether ineffectual; bleeding, purging, and cleansing medicines were vain; and the physicians were at their wit's end. *Jac Carpus*, a celebrated anatomist and surgeon at *Bologne*, had alone been master of the cure, which was by mercury administered to raise a salivation; he had attained this secret in his travels through *Spain* and *Italy*, and practised it for some years, and with such success and applause, that it is incredible what immense riches this one *nostrum* brought him (it is said upon good authority, that in one year he cleared six thousand pistoles) he acknowledged himself, that he did not know the end of his own wealth; for the captains, merchants, governors, commanders, &c. who had brought that filthy disease from *America*, were very well content to give him what sums he pleased to ask to free them from it.—*Paracelsus* about this time having likewise learnt the properties of mercury, and most likely from *Carpus*, who undertook the same cure but in a very different manner; for whereas *Carpus* did all by salivation—*Paracelsus* making up his preparation in pills attained his ends in a gentler manner. By this he informs us he cured the itch, leprosy, ulcers, *Naples* disease, and even gout, all which disorders were incurable on the foot of popular practice, and thus was the great basis laid for all his future fame and fortune.

Paracelsus, thus furnished with arts, and arrived at a degree of eminence beyond any of his brothers in the profession, was invited by the curators of the university of *Bazil* to the chair of professor of medicine and philosophy in that university. The art of printing was now a new thing, the taste for learning and art was warm*, and the magistracy of *Bazil* were very indus-

---

* We feel ourselves happy in being able to say, that the taste for learning and arts (notwithstanding the follies of the age) was never more prevalent than in the present time; the year 1801 commences an age of flourishing science, in which even our females seem to wish to bear a part—instance, a lady of quality, who went in her carriage the other day to Foster-lane, Cheapside, and bought a portable blacksmith's forge for her private amusement; her person was strong and athletic, and very fit for the manual practice of handling iron, and working other metallic experiments.

trious

trious in procuring professors of reputation from all parts of the world.   They had already got *Desid. Erasmus*, professor of *theology*, and *J. Oporinus* professor of the Greek tongue ; and now in 1527 *Paracelsus* was associated in the 33d year of his age.   Upon his first entrance into that province, having to make a public speech before the university, he posted up a very elegant advertisement over the doors inviting every body to his doctrine.   At his first lecture he ordered a brass vessel to be brought into the middle of the school, where after he had cast in sulphur and nitre, in a very solemn manner he burnt the books of *Galen* and *Avicenna*, alledging that he had held a dispute with them in the gates of hell, and had fairly routed and overcome them.   And hence he proclaimed, that the physicians should all follow him ; and no longer style themselves *Galenists*, but *Paracelsists*.—" Know," says he, " physicians, my cap has more learning in it than all your heads, my beard has more experience than your whole academies : Greeks, Latins, French, Germans, Italians, I will be your king."

While he was here professor he read his book *De Tartaro, de Gradibus*, and *De compositionibus*, in public lectures, to which he added a *commentary* on the book *De Gradibus* ; all these he afterwards printed at *Bazil* for the use of his disciples ; so that these must be allowed for genuine writings ; about the same time he wrote *De Calculo*, which performance *Helmont* speaks of with high approbation.

Notwithstanding his being professor in so learned an university he understood but a very little *Latin* ; his long travels, and application to business, and disuse of the language, had very much disqualified him for writing or speaking therein ; and his natural warmth rendered him very unfit for teaching at all.   Hence, though his auditors and disciples were at first very numerous, yet they very much fell off, and left him preaching to the walls. —In the mean time he abandoned himself to drinking at certain seasons ; *Oporinus*, who was always near him, has the good nature to say, he was never sober ; but that he tippled on from morning to night, and from night to morning, in a continual round.   At length he soon became weary of his professorship, and after three years continuance therein relinquished it, saying, that

no

no language besides the *German* was proper to reveal the secrets of chymistry in.

After this he again betook himself to an itinerant life, travelling and drinking, and living altogether at inns and taverns, continually flushed with liquor, and yet working many admirable cures in his way. In this manner he passed four years from the 43d to the 47th year of his life, when he died at an inn at *Saltzburg*, at the sign of the White Horse, on a bench in the chimney-corner. *Oporinus* relates, that after he had put on any new thing, it never came off his back till he had worn it into rags; he adds, that notwithstanding his excess in point of drinking, he was never addicted to venery.—But there is this reason for it : when he was a child, being neglected by his nurse, a *hag* gelded him in a place where three ways met, and so made a eunuch of him; accordingly in his writings he omits no opportunity of railing against women.—Such is the life of Paracelsus ; such is the immortal man, who sick of life retired into a corner of the world, and there supports himself with his own *Quintessence of Life.*

In his life time he only published three or four books, but after his death he grew prodigiously voluminous, scarce a year passing but one book or other was published under his name, said to be found in some old wall, ceiling, or the like. All the works published under his name were printed together at *Strasburg* in the year 1603, in three volumes *folio*, and again in 1616. *J. Oporinus*, that excellent professor and printer, before named, who constantly attended *Paracelsus* for three years as his menial servant, in hopes of learning some of his secrets, who published the works of *Vesalius*, and is supposed to have put them in that elegant language wherein they now appear : this *Oporinus*, in an epistle to *Monavius*, concerning the life of *Paracelsus*, professes himself surprized to find so many works of his master; for, that in all the time he was with him never wrote a word himself, nor ever took pen in hand, but forced *Oporinus* to write what he dictated; and *Oporinus* wondered much how such coherent words and discourse which might even become the wisest persons, should come from the mouth of a drunken man. His work

called

called *Archidoxa Medicinæ*, as containing the principles and maxims of the art, nine books of which were published at first; and the author in the prolegomena to them, speaks thus :—" *I intended to have published my ten books of* " *Archidoxa; but finding mankind unworthy of such a treasure as the tenth,* " *I keep it close in my* occiput, *and have firmly resolved never to bring it thence,* " *till you have all abjured* ARISTOTLE, AVICEN, *and* GALEN, *and have sworn* " *allegiance to* PARACELSUS *alone."*

However, the book did at length get abroad, though by what means is not known; it is undoubtedly an excellent piece, and may be ranked among the principal productions in the way of chymistry, that have ever appeared; whether or no it be *Paracelsus's* we cannot affirm, but there is one thing speaks in its behalf, *viz.* it contains a great many things which have since been trumped up for great *nostrums*; and *Van Helmont's* Lithonthriptic and Alcahest are apparently taken from hence; among the genuine writings of *Paracelsus* are likewise reckoned, that *De Ortu Rerum Naturalium, De Transformatione Rerum Naturalium,* and *De Vita Rerum Naturalium.* The rest are spurious or very doubtful, particularly his theological works.

The great fame and success of this man, which many attribute to his possessing an *universal medicine* may be accounted for from other principles. It is certain he was well acquainted with the use and virtue of *opium*, which the *Galenists* of those times all rejected as cold in the fourth degree. *Oporinus* relates that he made up certain little pills of the colour, figure, and size of mouse-turds, which were nothing but *opium.* These he called by a barbarous sort of name, his *laudanum; q. d.* laudable medicine; he always carried them with him, and prescribed them in dyssenteries, and all cases attended with intense pains, anxieties, deliriums, and obstinate wakings; but to be alone possessed of the use of so extraordinary and noble a medicament as *opium*, was sufficient to make him famous.

Another grand remedy with Paracelsus was *turbith mineral*; this is first mentioned in his *Clein Spital Boeck,* or *Chirurgia Minor,* where he gives the preparation.—In respect of the philosopher's stone *Oporinus* says, he often wondered to see him one day without a farthing in his pocket, and the next

day

day, full of money; that he took nothing with him when he went abroad. He adds, that he would often borrow money of his companions, the carmen and porters, and pay it again in twenty-four hours with extravagant interest, and yet from what fund nobody but himself knew. In the *Theatrum Alchemiæ* he mentions a treasure, hid under a certain tree; and from such like grounds they supposed him to possess the art of making gold; but it was hard if such noble nostrums as he possessed would not subsist him without the *lapis philosophorum*.

JOHN RUDOLPH GLAUBER.

J. R. GLAUBER, a celebrated chymist of *Amsterdam*, accounted the *Paracelsus* of his time: he had travelled much and by that means attained to a great many secrets. He wrote above thirty tracts, in some of which he acted the physician; in others, the adept; and in others, the metallist. He principally excelled in the last capacity, and alchymy.

He was a person of easy and genteel address, and, beyond dispute, well versed in chymistry: being author of the salt, still used in the shops, called *Sal Glauberi*; as also of all the salts, by oil of vitriol, *&c*. He is noted for extolling his arcanæ and preparations, and is reported to have traded unfairly with his secrets: the best of them he would sell, at excessive rates, to chymists and others, and would afterwards re-sell them, or make them public, to increase his fame; whence he was continually at variance with them.

The principal of his writings are *De Furnis*, and *De Metallis*, which, though wrote in *Dutch*, have been translated into *Latin* and *English*. It was *Glauber* who shewed, before the States of *Holland*, that there is gold contained in sand; and made an experiment thereof to their entire satisfaction: but so much

much lead, fire, and labour, being employed in procuring it, that the art would not pay charges *. However he plainly demonstrated, that there is no earth, sand, sulphur, or salt, or other matter, but what contains gold in a greater or less quantity. In short, he possessed a great many secrets, which are at this time in the hands of some of our modern chymists.

DOCTOR DEE, AND SIR EDWARD KELLY.

DOCTOR JOHN DEE, and SIR EDWARD KELLY, knight, being professed associates, their story is best delivered together. They have some title to the philosopher's stone in common fame. *Dee*, besides his being deep in chymistry, was very well versed in mathematics, particularly geometry and astrology : but Sir *Edward Kelly* appears to have been the leading man in alchymy. In some of *Dee*'s books are found short memoirs of the events of his operations : as, *Donum Dei*, five ounces. And in another place, " *This day* " Edward Kelly *discovered the grand secret to me, sit nomen Domini benedictum.*" *Ashmole* says, absolutely, they were masters of the powder of projection, and, with a piece not bigger than the smallest grain of sand, turned an ounce and a quarter of mercury into pure gold : but here is an equivoque; for granting them possessed of the powder of projection, it does not appear they had the secret of making it. The story is, that they found a considerable quantity of it in the ruins of *Glastonbury Abbey*, with which they performed many notable transmutations for the satisfaction of several persons. *Kelly*, in particular, is said to have given away rings of gold wire to the tune of 4000l. at the

---

* It has been asserted by several eminent chymists, that it might be performed to advantage, as the process is very simple, and takes up but little time : all that is requisite is silver, sand, and litharge.

marriage

marriage of his servant maid. And a piece of a brass warming-pan being cut out by order of queen *Elizabeth*, and sent to them when abroad, was returned pure gold. Likewise *Dee* made a present to the landgrave of *Hesse* of twelve *Hungarian* horses, which could never be expected from a man of his circumstances without some extraordinary means.

In the year 1591 they went into *Germany*, and settled some time at *Trebona*, in *Bohemia*; the design of which journey is very mysterious. Some say their design was to visit the alchymists of these countries, in order to get some light into the art of making the powder. Accordingly they travelled through *Poland, &c.* in quest thereof, and, some say, attained it; others say, not. Others, again, will make them sent by the queen as spies, and that alchymy was only a pretence, or means, to bring them into confidence with the people. But what will give most light upon this subject, is a book, now extant, wrote by *Dee*, entitled *Dee's Conferences with Spirits*, but some conjecture it to be with *Trithemius's* mere Cryptography; which light Doctor *Hook* takes it in. However, this book is truly curious in respect of the many magical operations there displayed, it being wrote journal-fashion by the Doctor's own hand, and relates circumstantially the conferences he held with some spirits (either good or bad) in company with Sir *Edward Kelly*.

They were no sooner gone out of *England* than *Dee's* library was opened by the queen's order, and 4000 books, and 700 choice manuscripts, were taken away on pretence of his being a conjuror. That princess soon after used means to bring him back again, which a quarrel with *Kelly* happening to promote, he returned in 1596, and in 1598 was made warden of *Manchester* college, where he died *.

Some very curious manuscripts, with the chrystal he used to invoke the spirits into, are at this time carefully laid up in the *British Museum*.†

---

* Authors differ very much in respect of the place where Doctor *Dee* resigned his life: it appears from the most eminent historians that he died at his house at *Mortlake*.

† Although *Dee's* manuscripts, and his Magic Chrystal, are to be seen at the Museum, there are six or seven individuals in *London* who assert they have the stone in their possession; thereby wishing to deceive the credulous, and to tempt them to a purchase at an enormous price.

As

As for Sir *Edward Kelly*, the Emperor, suspecting he had the secret of the philosophers in his possession, clapped him up in prison, in hopes to become a sharer in the profits of transmutation : however, *Kelly* defeated his intentions. After having been twice imprisoned, the last time he was shut up endeavouring to make his escape by means of the sheets of his bed tied together, they happened to slip the knots, and so let him fall, by which he broke his leg, and soon after lost his life.

THE CONCLUSION.

HAVING collected the most interesting and curious accounts of the lives of those great men, so famous for their speculations in philosophic learning, we draw to a conclusion ; having only to add, that we have sufficiently discovered in this biographical sketch whatsoever was necessary to prove the authenticity of *Our Art*, which we have delivered faithfully and impartially, noting, at the same time, the various opinions of different men at different ages ; likewise, we have taken sufficient trouble to explain what is meant by the word *Magic*, and to clear up the term from the imputation of any diabolical association with evil spirits, *&c.* Also, how nearly it is allied to our religious duties, we refer the reader to the annotations under the article *Zoroaster*, where we have spoke of the *Magi*, or wise men, proving the first who adored Christ were actually magicians. It is enough that we have spoke of the principal characters renowned in past ages for their laborious inquisition into the labyrinth of occult and natural philosophy ; there are many other philosophers standing upon ancient and modern record. A copious and general biography falls not within the limits of our work. We have introduced some characters (applicable to the subject before us) most distinguished for occult learning ; of which kind of science, whether by a particular influence of planetary configuration, which may have directed and impelled my mind and intellects to the observation and study of nature, and her simple operations, as well as to the more occult, I leave to the judgment of the astrologers, to whose inspection I submit a figure

of

of my nativity, which I shall annex to a sketch of my own history, which I mean to make the subject of a future publication, including a vast number of curious experiments in occult and chymical operations, which have fell either under my own observation, or have been transmitted to me from others. In respect of the astrologic art, (as we have already observed) it has such an affinity with talismanic experiments, &c. that no one can bring any work to a complete effect without a due knowledge and observation of the qualities and effects of the constellations (which occasioned us to give it the title of the Constellatory Art;) likewise, a man must be well acquainted with the nature, qualities, and effects, of the four elements, and of the animal, vegetable, and mineral kingdoms; which knowledge cannot better be obtained than by chymical experience, for it does, as I may say, unlock the secret chambers of nature, and introduces the student into a world of knowledge, which could not be attained but by chymical analyzation, whereby we decompound mixt bodies, and reduce them to their simple natures, and come to a thorough acquaintance with those powerful and active principles, causing the wonderful transmutations of one compound body into another of a different species, as is to be seen in the course of our operations upon salts and metals, giving us clear and comprehensive ideas of the principles of life or generation, and putrefaction or death.

Finally, to conclude, we are chiefly to consider one thing to be attained as the ground of perfection in the rest: *i. e.* The great *First Cause*, the *Eternal Wisdom*, to know the Creator by the contemplation of the creature. This is the grand secret of the philosophers, and the master-key to all sciences both human and divine, for without this we are still wandering in a labyrinth of perplexity and errors, of darkness and obscurity: for this is the sum and perfection of all learning, to live in the fear of God, and in love and charity with all men.

FINIS.